Keeping America Working: Profiles in Partnership

Philip R. Day, Jr.
Koosappa Rajasekhara

70142

American Association of Community and Junior Colleges
National Center for Higher Education
Suite 410, One Dupont Circle, NW
Washington, D.C. 20036
(202) 293-7050

TABLE OF CONTENTS

FOREWORD

One of the most dynamic activities over the past decade within the world of community, technical, and junior colleges has been the growth of collaborative arrangements between local employers and community colleges. The vitality of this development is so rich that it could best be described as "a movable feast."

Only once before in the history of American higher education has there been such a strong linkage between the nation's employer community and a significant arm of higher education. The signing and implementation of the Morrill Act ushered in the first landmark partnership between higher education and the nation's economic needs—in this case, the need of a nation to feed itself independently. The birth of the "land grant" colleges and the extension agent concept is one of the great American success stories.

With much less fanfare and federal direction, a second momentous partnership is being created between the nation's employer community and an important segment of the higher education community. This partnership ultimately will rival the land grant college initiative in terms of economic impact and societal impact. The collaboration between community, technical, and junior colleges and employers will do for adult working Americans, in the information age, what land grant colleges did for farmers in an agriculture-industrial age.

Pat Choate, assistant to the president, TRW, recently stated that the driving force behind the future American economy will be trade, technology, and demography. The rule of the day will be massive and continuous changes in the work place and for the work force, he said, and the ease and success with which the American work force negotiates such changes will largely depend upon the accessibility and utilization of employee education and training.

Employers and community colleges are presently forging a substantial series of simple and complex partnerships aimed at creating and maintaining a highly skilled and flexible labor force. The demographics tell us that the present work force is essentially the same labor pool at the nation's disposal through the year 2020. Therefore, the development unfolding is largely an invention of necessity. Employers are urgently seeking consistent and qualitative education and training delivery systems in order to maintain their competitive edge. Increasingly, as a reflection of a community's desire for economic stability and growth, community, technical, and junior colleges are becoming the preferred education resource for employers and employees alike.

The difficulty with the rapid growth of these new relationships is that a description of the "state of the art" becomes a challenge. The problem is akin to attempting a picture of a moving train—the result will be a picture of where the train was. Nonetheless, a picture of the status of college/employer partnerships remains an important objective.

This is not a thorough research of partnerships, but rather a selected inventory of practices in institutions we chose as a result of a track record of exemplary practices in this area. The results, therefore, should be used as indicators and objects of research, not as data that can be applied to the entire community college network.

This inventory is a necessary first step in a more systematic study of the texture of the phenomenon of partnerships. The exercise has been valuable in terms of information revealed and not revealed. Perhaps the greatest service of the inventory has been alerting everyone involved in it to the difficulty of greater research in this area. The colleges are simply so busy responding and delivering services to employers that they have not always documented their processes. Sometimes the documentation is present, but it is not organized under a single source. The inventory has highlighted this problem. The Department of Education has played a key role in helping document the landscape and is stimulating procedural improvement.

Special thanks for this report go to Dr. Philip R. Day, Jr., president of Dundalk Community College, Dundalk, Maryland, senior author of this monograph. Thanks, too, go to Koosappa Rajasekhara, director of institutional research and grants at the college, who conducted the research and prepared the data.

> Dale Parnell
> President
> American Association of Community
> and Junior Colleges

PREFACE

This report presents an analysis of a survey of selected community, technical, and junior colleges in the nation that are active in developing and marketing college/business partnerships. The purpose of the survey was to broaden the knowledge base of the last business/industry survey, conducted during 1984. This extensive industry training study provides valuable information for pursuing private sector, congressional, and federal agency support for the expansion of such training programs at two-year institutions.

It is the fourth in a series of reports published by the American Association of Community and Junior Colleges on comparative ventures between community, technical, and junior colleges and the private sector. Earlier reports are *Putting America Back to Work: The Kellogg Leadership Initiative; In Search of Community College Partnerships;* and *Directory of Business/Industry Coordinators.*

The first publication outlined current and future roles for community colleges in economic and human resource development. The second revealed the extent to which the colleges participate in Private Industry Councils, offer employee training in both the public and private sectors, provide support to small businesses, and collaborate with economic development offices. The last lists 421 two-year colleges with business/industry liaison offices.

As was the case in earlier reports, this project was undertaken in cooperation with the American Association of Community and Junior Colleges (AACJC) and the Association of Community College Trustees (ACCT) in conjunction with the Keeping America Working project. Association staff members James F. Gollattscheck, James Mahoney, James F. McKenney, Mary Ann Settlemire, Jeannie Hickman, and Valerie L. Brooks were specifically helpful in the analysis and editing stage of the project. Special thanks go to the staff of Dundalk Community College's Office of Institutional Research and Grants for assisting in the project. Thanks, too, go to James L. Smith, director of Data Processing at Essex Community College, who assisted in the initial analysis of this data.

Philip R. Day, Jr.
Director of the Study and President
Dundalk Community College

EXECUTIVE SUMMARY

An inventory of selected community, technical, and junior colleges, in cooperation with the American Association of Community and Junior Colleges (AACJC) and the Association of Community College Trustees (ACCT), was conducted to gain an in-depth knowledge of business/industry training programs provided by these colleges. The results of this study supplement earlier work completed by the senior author and provide additional insights into the dimensions of community, technical, and junior college partnerships with local business and industry.

Survey results also help to quantify more specifically the extent and range of efforts conducted by local two-year colleges that are designed to improve the quality of the work force and the efficiency of public and private enterprises. The highlights of the findings are presented below.

GENERAL NOTATIONS

- The overall response rate was 75 percent, with 54 out of 72 selected colleges responding to the inventory.
- More than half of the responding institutions serve urban areas, and 35 percent serve suburban districts. Half of the responding institutions reported that more than 50 percent of their students were enrolled in occupational/technical curricula. Urban and suburban institutions reported that 61 to 70 percent of the credit student population were part-time and the same percentage range applied to students who were employed. Only one-third of all students in these institutions were under the age of 21.
- Almost all institutions reported participation in work-related programs for which students were awarded academic credit. The participation rates varied from 28 percent in the National Guide for Training Program to 90 percent participation in cooperative education.
- Eight out of 10 institutions reported offering between 1 and 20 credits for work-related experience.

CORPORATE ORGANIZATIONAL PROFILE

- More than half of the urban institutions, one-third of the suburban institutions, and just over one-tenth of the rural institutions reported that the industries located in their areas were international in scope. The same proportional distribution was reported for national and regionally based corporations.

MILITARY CONTRACTS

- Forty-two percent of all institutions reported that they offered educational training programs for military personnel. Of these, 58 percent of urban, 30 percent of suburban, and 17 percent of rural institutions engaged in such training activities. College charges for individual educational training contracts for military personnel training programs varied from $2,000 to nearly $950,000.

BUSINESS/INDUSTRY/COLLEGE COLLABORATION

- The average number of firms involved in industry/college partnership training programs with individual colleges ranged annually from a low of 40 for rural institutions to a high of 530 for urban institutions.
- Over 28,000 employees took job-related courses in one year in the responding colleges. An overwhelming majority (21,562) of these employees were trained by urban institutions.
- Half of the urban and suburban institutions and two-thirds of rural institutions reported that employees taking job-related courses were fully subsidized by their employers.
- Fifty-eight percent of all institutions reported that companies granted work-release time for their employees who took courses through the colleges.

COURSE/INSTRUCTIONAL PROFILE

- Over 650 different courses/programs were offered by the colleges to employees of their area industries.
- Eighty-seven percent of the institutions reported offering the courses/programs either at the plant or on the college campus. The majority were offered off-campus.

TRAINING INVOLVING JTPA AND OTHER OUTSIDE FUNDING

- Nearly 20,000 people participated in training programs supported by the Job Training Partnership Act (JTPA) and other outside funding provided by the colleges.
- Ninety-six percent of the participants in these programs attended urban and suburban institutions.
- Nearly $15 million was received by the colleges to support the training program. About three-fourths of this amount came from JTPA. Urban and suburban institutions shared almost equally 96 percent of the JTPA funds.

TYPICAL COLLEGE PARTNERSHIP BY LOCATION

Below are sketches of typical urban, suburban, and rural colleges and their partnerships based upon data collected through this survey.

	Urban Colleges	Suburban Colleges	Rural Colleges
A. College Data			
1. Credit headcount	10,000	10,000 +	1,000–5,000
2. % credit headcount in occupational/technical	40	40	14
3. % ethnic minorities	30–40	10–20	10–20
4. % part-time students	30–40	30–40	50–60
5. % employed	30–40	30–40	50–60
6. % female	51–60	51–60	41–50
7. % students between 22–40 years old	43–70	33–60	33–60
8. Noncredit headcount/% in technical education	5,000 + /20	1,000–5,000/40	1,000/20
9. Number of technical education degree programs	40–60	30	30–40
10. Technical education curriculum advisory committees	yes	yes	yes
B. College/Business Partnership Detail			
1. Most popular business-selected courses	office occupations electronics management	office occupations electronics management	office occupations electronics management

Continued

TYPICAL COLLEGE PARTNERSHIP BY LOCATION *(continued)*

	Urban Colleges	Suburban Colleges	Rural Colleges
2. Most popular special program partnerships	accounting data processing industrial management cooperative ed., nonapprenticeship	accounting data processing industrial management cooperative ed., apprenticeship, nonapprenticeship	accounting data processing law enforcement cooperative ed., apprenticeship, nonapprenticeship, military
3. Average number of partnerships annually	30	15	6–7
4. Average number of employee-students yearly	2,000	270	270
5. Company funding for programs/release time (rt)	full funding/rt college for both	full funding/rt company/ equip/ college material	full funding/rt company for both
6. Sources of training equipment and curriculum material			
7. Sources of training faculty	college faculty	noncompany, part-time faculty	college faculty
8. Credit toward AA/certificate for training prog.	yes	yes	no
9. Average number of JTPA programs annually	7–8	4–5	3
10. Average number of students/ JTPA program	530	105	75
11. Average size of JTPA grant/ contact	$34,638	$77,360	$7,500

INTRODUCTION

In a recently published report by the Carnegie Foundation, *Higher Education and the American Resurgence,* Frank Newman commented that in "every region of the country, states are struggling to bolster their economies. More than 30 state commissions have reported their findings. The same themes run through these reports. The time has come, they say, to:

- Accelerate economic growth and job information
- Attract advanced technology industry
- Improve elementary and secondary education in order to improve the skills of the work force
- Invest in the research universities in order to improve the research base and the numbers of technically trained graduates
- Create links between business and the colleges and business and the schools." (Newman, 1985)

What has become obvious is that the educational system has become a central focus of concern and a major element of a renewed strategy that attempts to improve our competitive position in the international marketplace. Each component within the national education system has its important function and role to play. Dale Parnell, president of the American Association of Community and Junior Colleges (AACJC), suggests that until recently one of the least recognized (and consequently undervalued) components in this system was the community, technical, and junior college network that exists nationwide. "The community, technical, and junior colleges have a special role to play in the economic vitalization of the United States. Their mission places them squarely in the service of local communities—their businesses, their public agencies, their schools, and their cultural and social groups and organizations. For years they have provided education, technical assistance, and community service programs designed to meet the needs of the communities. In the last few years, when the central issue in the nation was the economy, the colleges redoubled their efforts to work with local employers (both public and private) to train employees to handle new machines, new processes, and new jobs; the colleges increased their education and training services for government agencies and other public enterprises; they offered a variety of technical assistance to the districts they serve; [and] they coordinated their academic and training programs with those offered by area high schools. In so doing, they established themselves as significant participants in the economic development plans of local communities." (Day, 1985)

How significant this role has been and will potentially be had not been systematically researched on a national level until the study entitled *In*

Search of Community College Partnerships was completed. The results of this study confirmed that community colleges have been and are currently playing a major role in economic development at the local, state, regional, and national levels. Over 770 institutions responded to this study and provided specific information on programmatic, structural, and organizational trends relating to businesses and high school partnerships. A copy of the executive summary of this study is included in the Appendix of this report (see Appendix A).

While providing us with valued information, the study had some limitations, given its scope and timetable. It did not give us specific information on the details of operationalizing the linkages, ways to make them work effectively, and the impact (positive or negative) that they had on the local colleges and the communities served by these institutions.

In an effort to broaden the knowledge gained by the community college partnership study, an in-depth follow up inventory of selected institutions was conducted by Dundalk Community College for AACJC/ACCT during 1985. It was expected that this study would provide more "details" about these current trends. When coupled with the comprehensive view of business/industry/college partnerships generated by the first study, it provides invaluable information for current practitioners and assists AACJC/ACCT in their pursuit of national, state, and local support for education/training and other funds. It also was expected that a thorough evaluation of this study would assist AACJC/ACCT to determine future directions and requirements for technical assistance that could be provided by these associations.

Specific areas addressed in this follow-up survey were:
A. General and Demographic Information on Both Credit and Noncredit Students
B. Technical and Vocational Programs
C. Transfer Programs
D. Community Economic Profile
E. Corporate Organizational Profile
F. Military Contracts
G. Business/Industry/College Collaboration
H. Course/Instructional Profile
I. Training Involving Funding under the Job Training Partnership Act (JTPA)

METHODOLOGY

STUDY POPULATION

The study population consisted of 72 selected community, technical, and junior colleges across the United States. (For a listing of respondents, see Appendix B.) The selection of the colleges was based on geographic and racial distribution as well as the degree to which business/industry partnerships existed among the colleges. A concerted effort was made to choose a sample of colleges with strong reputations in business/industry collaborations. Most of the colleges had participated in the previous AACJC/ACCT-sponsored national study (Day, 1984).

Additionally, several institutions were included in the study that had not participated in the earlier effort. In such cases, the inventory and cover letter were mailed directly to the college president. The president also received follow-up phone calls to reinforce the importance of the inventory. After a follow-up mailing and telephone call, usable returns were received from 54 of the 72 colleges. This gave a return rate of 75 percent.

SURVEY INSTRUMENT AND PROCEDURE

The inventory was developed by AACJC and the staff of Dundalk Community College (see Appendix C). The inventory consisted of items concerning enrollment, demographic and programmatic areas, community economic profiles, corporate profiles, and employment data. These items were not included in a previous survey (Day, 1984). The inventory was mailed to the business/industry coordinators who had completed the 1984 survey with a cover letter from the president of AACJC explaining the study and asking their cooperation and assistance in completing the inventory form.

DATA ANALYSIS

The data were analyzed using the *Statistical Package for Social Sciences* (SPSS) (Nie, Hull, Jenkins, Steinbrenner, and Brent, 1975, and Nie and Hull, 1981). Responses were cross-tabulated with respect to the primary location of the college: urban, suburban, and rural. Also, the overall frequency of responses was obtained. A few cases in each analysis had to be discarded due to missing data.

FINDINGS

GENERAL

Apart from the institutional identification and the name of the staff person completing the survey, the general informational category included such areas as enrollment, sex, race, age, and employment for both credit and noncredit students. In terms of the original inventory pool the breakdown was as follows:

Urban—51%
Suburban—35%
Rural—14%

The breakdown of responding colleges was as follows:

Urban—47%
Suburban—40%
Rural—13%

The urban colleges responded at a lower rate than their composition in the original pool, while suburban institutions responded at a 5 percent higher rate than their representation in the original selection.

CREDIT ENROLLMENT

Headcount
One-half of all responding institutions reported a headcount enrollment of over 10,000 (Table 1). Nearly two-thirds of urban institutions, 43 percent of the suburban institutions, and 14 percent of rural institutions enrolled over 10,000 students. An overwhelming majority (86 percent)

TABLE 1
CREDIT HEADCOUNT ENROLLMENT BY LOCATION
(IN PERCENT)

HEADCOUNT	URBAN	SUBURBAN	RURAL	AVERAGE
501–1,000	-	4.8	-	1.9
1,001–5,000	24.0	28.6	85.7	32.7
5,001–10,000	12.0	23.8	-	15.4
Over 10,000	64.0	42.8	14.3	50.0
TOTAL	47.2	39.6	13.2	100.0
NO. OF RESPONDENTS	25	21	7	53

of rural institutions had headcount enrollments of between 1,000 and 5,000. The disparity in these figures again points to the basic difference in the three communities. Urban and suburban institutions in this sample were comparable in size of enrollment, both substantially higher than enrollment in rural colleges.

Full-Time Equivalent (FTE)

In terms of full-time equivalents (FTEs), over one-half (52 percent) of all urban institutions, about a third (35 percent) of suburban, and less than a fifth (17 percent) of rural institutions reported credit FTEs of more than 5,000 (Table 2). Less than half of the suburban institutions had less than 3,000 FTEs. As might be anticipated, only about one-fourth of the urban institutions registered less than 3,000 FTEs. Again, these figures reinforce the size differential among the three types of community colleges. Size and the composition of that size can be an important variable in terms of the symbiotic relationship that is possible between a college and its community. The FTE range for urban institutions was between 1,500 and 27,000; for suburban institutions, it was between 600 and 13,000; and for rural institutions the range was between 1,000 and 6,100 FTEs.

TABLE 2
CREDIT FTE ENROLLMENT BY LOCATION
(IN PERCENT)

FULL-TIME EQUIVALENT	URBAN	SUBURBAN	RURAL	AVERAGE
1–1,999	9.5	30.0	33.3	21.3
2,000–2,999	14.3	15.0	33.3	17.0
3,000–4,999	24.0	20.0	16.7	21.3
5,000–9,999	28.4	20.0	16.7	23.3
10,000–14,999	14.3	15.0	-	13.0
15,000–19,999	-	-	-	-
Over 20,000	9.5	-	-	4.1
TOTAL	44.5	42.5	13.0	100.0
NO. OF RESPONDENTS	21	20	6	47
FTE RANGE	1,526–27,142	614–12,758	1,038–6,086	-

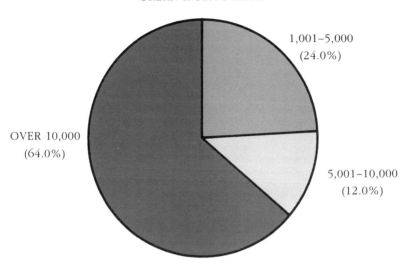

FIGURE 1
CREDIT HEADCOUNT ENROLLMENT
URBAN INSTITUTIONS

1,001–5,000
(24.0%)

OVER 10,000
(64.0%)

5,001–10,000
(12.0%)

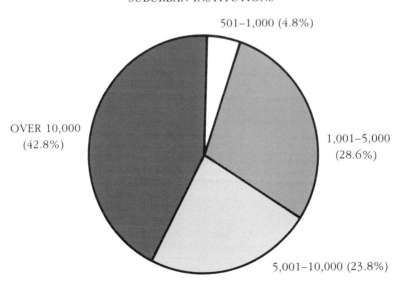

FIGURE 2
CREDIT HEADCOUNT ENROLLMENT
SUBURBAN INSTITUTIONS

501–1,000 (4.8%)

OVER 10,000
(42.8%)

1,001–5,000
(28.6%)

5,001–10,000 (23.8%)

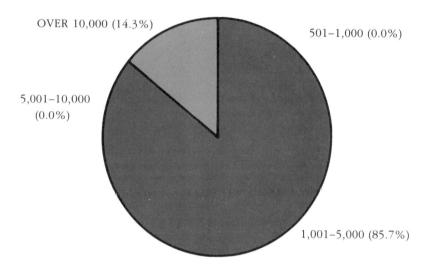

FIGURE 3
CREDIT HEADCOUNT ENROLLMENT
RURAL INSTITUTIONS

OVER 10,000 (14.3%)

501–1,000 (0.0%)

5,001–10,000
(0.0%)

1,001–5,000 (85.7%)

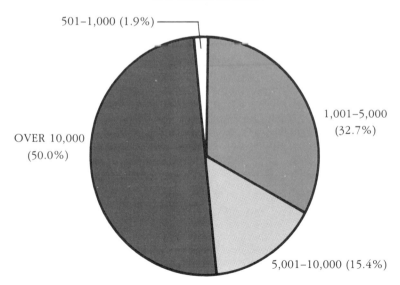

FIGURE 4
CREDIT HEADCOUNT ENROLLMENT
ALL INSTITUTIONS

501–1,000 (1.9%)

1,001–5,000
(32.7%)

OVER 10,000
(50.0%)

5,001–10,000 (15.4%)

Enrollment in Occupational/Technical Courses

Over one-half of all responding institutions reported that more than 51 percent of their student bodies had enrolled in occupational/technical courses (Table 3). According to the survey, more students in suburban and rural institutions were taking occupational courses than those enrolled in urban institutions. It appeared that the students in the urban institutions were more liberal arts- and transfer-oriented than those in other institutions.

TABLE 3

PERCENT OF CREDIT STUDENTS TAKING OCCUPATIONAL
COURSES BY LOCATION
(IN PERCENT)

PERCENT	URBAN	SUBURBAN	RURAL	TOTAL
1–20	-	5.0	14.3	3.9
21–30	16.7	5.0	-	9.8
31–40	12.5	5.0	14.3	9.8
41–50	29.2	20.0	14.2	23.5
51–60	16.6	25.0	28.6	21.6
Over 60	25.0	40.0	28.6	31.4
TOTAL	47.1	39.2	13.7	100.0
NO. OF RESPONDENTS	24	20	7	51

Enrollment by Race

The racial distribution among rural and suburban institutions was somewhat similar. In these institutions, Caucasian students comprised between 81 and 90 percent of total credit headcount; black and other racial groups ranged from 1 to 10 percent each (Table 4). In urban institutions, between 61 and 70 percent were Caucasian, between 11 and 20 percent were black, and the remaining were distributed among other racial groups.

TABLE 4

CREDIT ENROLLMENT BY RACE BY LOCATION
(IN PERCENT)

RACE	URBAN	SUBURBAN	RURAL	TOTAL
Caucasian	61–70	81–90	81–90	71–80
Black	11–20	1–10	1–10	1–10
Hispanic	1–10	1–10	1–10	1–10
Native American	1–10	1–10	1–10	1–10
Asian American	1–10	1–10	1–10	1–10
TOTAL	47.1	39.2	13.7	100.0
NO. OF RESPONDENTS	24	20	7	51

Enrollment by Full-Time and Part-Time

About two-thirds of the enrollment at the responding institutions were part-time, according to the survey (Table 5). In rural institutions, part-time enrollment was between 41 and 50 percent compared to between 61 and 70 percent among urban and suburban institutions.

TABLE 5

CREDIT ENROLLMENT BY STATUS BY LOCATION
(IN PERCENT)

STATUS	URBAN	SUBURBAN	RURAL	TOTAL
Part-time	61–70	61–70	41–50	66.9
Full-time	31–40	31–40	51–60	33.1
TOTAL	50.0	39.6	10.4	100.0
NO. OF RESPONDENTS	24	19	5	48

Employment

Nearly two-thirds of the student bodies in the institutions reporting (16 of 53) were employed (Table 6). Responding colleges reflected a student employment rate that was a mirror image of full-time/part-time status. The overall employment rate among the students in urban and suburban institutions was between 61 and 70 percent, while among the students in rural institutions it was between 41 and 50 percent. Of those who were employed, more than half (56 percent) were employed part-time. A higher percentage (61–70 percent) of students in urban institutions were employed full-time than those in suburban (41–50 percent) and rural (31–40 percent) institutions.

TABLE 6

CREDIT STUDENT EMPLOYMENT BY LOCATION
(IN PERCENT)

EMPLOYED	URBAN	SUBURBAN	RURAL	TOTAL
Total employed	61–70	61–70	41–50	66.3
Full-time	61–70	41–50	31–40	44.3
Part-time	41–50	41–50	51–60	55.7
TOTAL	50.0	37.5	12.5	100.0
NO. OF RESPONDENTS	8	6	2	16

Enrollment by Gender

The overall enrollment of women in the responding institutions was slightly higher than males. Nearly 51 percent of the student bodies was female and 49 percent male (Table 7). Among rural institutions, the percentage of male students was higher (51–60 percent) than female students

(41–50 percent). Alternatively, the percentage of females was higher at urban (51–60 percent) and suburban sites (51–60 percent).

TABLE 7
CREDIT ENROLLMENT BY GENDER BY LOCATION
(IN PERCENT)

SEX	URBAN	SUBURBAN	RURAL	TOTAL
Male	41–60	41–50	51–60	49.2
Female	51–60	51–60	41–50	50.8
TOTAL	49.0	37.3	13.7	100.0
NO. OF RESPONDENTS	25	19	7	51

Age Distribution

Only one-third of all credit students were under 21 years of age (Table 8). Nearly 40 percent of the students attending the community colleges were between the ages of 22 and 30 years. Students under 21 who were enrolled in rural institutions constituted between 41 and 50 percent of the total enrollment of those colleges.

The average age of urban students was 29 compared to 28 years for suburban and 27 for rural students. The larger percentage of students under 21 in rural institutions tended to lower the overall average age of the student. Many students in urban and suburban areas often attend colleges to update skills or change careers, which might explain the age differences. On the other hand, one could anticipate a more traditional approach in a rural setting where college pre-work education/training would be generally considered the last stop in the educational ladder.

TABLE 8
AGE DISTRIBUTION OF CREDIT STUDENTS
(IN PERCENT)

AGE INTERVAL	URBAN	SUBURBAN	RURAL	TOTAL
Under 21	21–30	21–30	41–50	31.0
22–25	21–30	11–20	11–20	24.0
26–30	11–20	11–20	11–20	15.0
31–40	11–20	11–20	11–20	15.0
41–50	1–10	1–10	1–10	5.0
51–60	1–10	1–10	1–10	5.0
Over 60	1–10	1–10	1–10	5.0
TOTAL	54.5	36.4	9.1	100.0
NO. OF RESPONDENTS	24	16	4	44
AVERAGE AGE	29	28	27	28

NONCREDIT ENROLLMENT

There were six items pertaining to the noncredit area. For the most part, the information for these items was not furnished by the institutions. Except for headcount enrollment and enrollment in occupational courses, the items were either left blank or noted "Not Available." It appears that institutions did not document their noncredit activities with the same zeal as their credit enrollments, probably because the funding mechanism of public institutions places credit courses at a distinct advantage in terms of state funding. However, it is important to note that the enrollment future lies in the noncredit area, especially for training.

NONCREDIT HEADCOUNT

More than half of all institutions reported a noncredit enrollment of 5,000 or fewer (Table 9). Three-fourths of rural institutions reported an enrollment of 1,000 or less. In contrast, more than half (57 percent) of urban institutions had a noncredit enrollment of more than 5,000. One-quarter of all urban institutions had a noncredit enrollment over 15,000.

TABLE 9
NONCREDIT HEADCOUNT ENROLLMENT BY LOCATION
(IN PERCENT)

INTERVAL	URBAN	SUBURBAN	RURAL	TOTAL
1–1,000	4.3	17.6	75.0	15.9
1,001–5,000	39.2	52.9	-	40.9
5,001–10,000	26.1	17.6	25.0	22.7
10,001–15,000	4.3	-	-	2.3
15,001 & Over	26.1	11.9	-	18.2
TOTAL	52.3	38.6	9.1	100.0
NO. OF RESPONDENTS	23	17	4	44

NONCREDIT ENROLLMENT IN OCCUPATIONAL/TECHNICAL COURSES

Just over one-third of all institutions reported that between 10 and 20 percent of their noncredit student body had enrolled in occupational/technical courses (Table 10). All rural institutions reported noncredit enrollment in this range (10–20 percent). Nearly 50 percent of the urban and 25 percent of suburban institutions reported that noncredit registration in vocational courses exceeded 41 percent. About 13 percent of both the urban and suburban institutions reported that over 61 percent of their noncredit students had enrolled in technical/occupational courses. There was no figure for rural colleges in this area.

TABLE 10

NONCREDIT ENROLLMENT IN OCCUPATIONAL COURSES
BY LOCATION (IN PERCENT)

PERCENT RANGE	URBAN	SUBURBAN	RURAL	TOTAL
10–20	33.3	25.0	100.0	36.0
21–30	6.7	12.5	-	8.0
31–40	13.3	37.5	-	20.0
41–50	26.7	-	-	16.0
51 60	6.7	12.5	-	8.0
61 & Over	13.3	12.5	-	12.0
TOTAL	61.5	30.8	7.7	100.0
NO. OF RESPONDENTS	15	8	2	25

Occupational Programs

The institutions were asked to respond to five questions under the occupational programs. The questions pertained to: numbers of programs offered, industrial advisory committee for degree programs, programs enrolling greatest numbers of employees from given firms, information on work-related experience, and the maximum number of credits allowed for such work-related experiential learning.

OCCUPATIONAL PROGRAMS LEADING TO AA DEGREE OR CERTIFICATE

Fifty-one percent of all institutions reported offering up to 30 different degree programs. More than one-half of all responding urban institutions reported that they offered over 41 different degree programs, while only one-fifth of suburban and rural institutions offered this number (Table 11). In contrast, nearly 40 percent of suburban and rural institutions reported offering between 1 and 20 programs, and 13 percent of urban institutions offered programs between this range.

TABLE 11
OCCUPATIONAL PROGRAMS LEADING TO AA DEGREE BY LOCATION (IN PERCENT)

NUMBER OF PROGRAMS	URBAN	SUBURBAN	RURAL	TOTAL
1–20	13.0	38.1	40.0	26.5
21–30	21.7	33.3	-	24.5
31–40	13.0	9.5	40.0	14.3
41–50	13.0	4.8	20.0	10.2
51–60	39.1	14.3	-	24.5
TOTAL	46.9	42.9	10.2	100.0
NO. OF RESPONDENTS	23	21	5	49

Fifty-four percent of the responding institutions reported offering between 1 and 20 certificate programs (Table 12). In contrast, only 27 percent of the institutions offered degree programs in this range. About 8 out of 10 of the suburban and rural institutions reported offering between 1 and 30 certificate programs, while 2 out of 3 of the suburban institutions offered programs in this range.

TABLE 12

OCCUPATIONAL PROGRAMS LEADING TO CERTIFICATE
BY LOCATION (IN PERCENT)

NUMBER OF PROGRAMS	URBAN	SUBURBAN	RURAL	TOTAL
1–20	41.7	68.4	20.0	54.2
21–30	12.5	10.5	60.0	12.5
31–40	12.5	5.3	-	8.3
41–50	12.5	10.5	20.0	12.5
51–60	20.8	5.3	-	12.5
TOTAL	50.0	39.6	10.4	100.0
NO. OF RESPONDENTS	24	19	5	48

Again, the data support the notion that the urban institutions, in either degree or certificate programs, are responding to their employer diversity with a program diversity to match. However, the important item in this section is the institutional flexibility represented by all the respondents in terms of certificate programs. These institutions are providing the shortest turn-around time possible for student and employer alike when it comes to pre-service or on-the-job education. Institutions in the 1–20 program range are offering certificates at almost double the rate for the same range in degree programs. This may be one of the critical reasons why the number of students in the 22–40 age bracket is so high. Certificate programs represent a "no frills" approach to education that appears to be the desired option for the older student.

INDUSTRIAL ADVISORY COMMITTEES

An overwhelming majority (94 percent) of the institutions reported that they had established industrial advisory committees for their degree programs (Table 13). Among these, urban and suburban institutions reported having a higher percentage (95–96 percent) of program advisory committees than institutions located in rural areas (83 percent).

TABLE 13

DEGREE PROGRAMS HAVING ADVISORY COMMITTEES BY LOCATION
(IN PERCENT)

ADVISORY COMMITTEE	URBAN	SUBURBAN	RURAL	TOTAL
Yes	95.7	95.0	83.3	93.9
No	4.3	5.0	16.7	6.1
TOTAL	46.9	40.8	12.3	100.0
NO. OF RESPONDENTS	23	20	6	49

PROGRAMS ENROLLING GREATEST NUMBER OF EMPLOYEES FROM GIVEN FIRMS

The most popular courses reported by the colleges (based on highest enrollment levels) were electronics and data processing. In each case, six institutions listed those as courses requested by the businesses and industries they serve. Again, these data show that the colleges and the students react to the job trends in their communities. The overall attractiveness of electronics and data processing is also a reflection of national trends in these growth areas. The programs varied from the traditional secretarial/word processor training to agribusiness, micro-electronics, health sciences, and a variety of industrial training programs. An analysis (by type of institution) to show the most common courses offered to local business and industry revealed the following: (1) rural institutions offered secretarial science, electronics, data processing, law enforcement, etc.; (2) suburban institutions offered electronics, data processing, management, nursing, accounting, mechanical engineering technology, industrial maintenance, etc.; (3) urban institutions offered office occupations, electronics, management, accounting, fire technology, etc. It appears that the most common programs for all three types of institutions were electronics, office occupations (secretarial science), management, and accounting. Appendix D includes a complete list of unduplicated courses offered by the participating institutions.

> Question #21—What occupational degree programs enroll the greatest numbers of employees from given firms? List four or five.

Courses with Highest Employee Enrollments

URBAN

Office Occupations (4)*
Electronics (3)
Management (3)
Accounting
Agribusiness
Public Service Institute
Industrial Electricity
Business Administration
Data Processing
Semiconductor Processing
Wastewater Management
Automotive

SUBURBAN

Electronics (6)
Data Processing (6)
Management (5)
Nursing (4)
Accounting (3)
Mechanical Engineering
   Technology (3)
Instrumentation (2)
Industrial Maintenance (2)
Computer Science (2)
Logistics
Machine Processing

Continued

Courses with Highest Employee Enrollments *(continued)*

URBAN	SUBURBAN
Banking	Automotive
Environmental Health	Lift Truck Certification
Technology	Electrical Engineering
Diesel Mechanics	Technology
Aviation Maintenance	Police Services
Nursing	Criminal Justice
Fire Technology	Secretarial Science
Respiratory Therapy	Machinist
Drafting	Welding
Microcomputer Training	Tourism

RURAL

Electronics (3)
Secretarial Science (2)
Law Enforcement (2)
Data Processing (2)
Accounting
Mechanical Technology
Business Administration
Nursing
Computer Science
Industrial Management

*Numbers within parentheses indicate the frequency with which course titles were identified by responding colleges.

AWARDING CREDIT FOR WORK-RELATED EXPERIENCE

The institutions were asked to identify their participation in a number of courses on work-related experiential learning. These were: cooperative education, work-study, National Guide for Training Program, apprenticeship program training, nonapprenticeship industry training, and military training (Table 14). Almost all responding institutions had participated in one, two, or all of the programs. The participation rates among the institutions in these programs varied from as low as 28 percent in National Guide for Training Program to a high of nearly 90 percent in cooperative education. It is interesting to note that apprenticeship programs, nonapprenticeship industry training, and military training are awarded credit at above the 50 percent level by colleges in all areas.

The area of credit for work-related experience is an important indicator of how well institutions are responding to the realities of the older and more experienced student. Credit for work experience is an attempt

16

by colleges to recognize and incorporate the students' knowledge base brought to the first registration.

TABLE 14
AWARDING CREDIT FOR WORK-RELATED EXPERIENCE
BY LOCATION (IN PERCENT)

PROGRAMS	URBAN	SUBURBAN	RURAL	TOTAL
Coop Education	95.5	81.0	100.0	89.8
Work-Study	38.1	29.4	40.0	34.9
National Guide for Training Program	42.1	12.5	20.0	27.5
Apprenticeship Program Training	47.6	62.5	80.0	56.8
Nonapprenticeship Industry Training	52.4	64.7	80.0	56.8
Military Training	77.3	52.9	83.3	68.9
TOTAL	44.9	42.9	12.2	100.0
NO. OF RESPONDENTS	22	21	6	49

COOPERATIVE EDUCATION

- Institutions located in rural areas reported 100 percent participation in cooperative education. Suburban institutions had the lowest participation rate of 81 percent, while urban colleges had nearly 96 percent participation.

WORK-STUDY

- Just over one-third of all institutions reported participation in work-study programs. Of these, rural institutions had a 40 percent participation rate, urban colleges had a 38.1 percent participation rate, while suburban institutions had a 29 percent participation rate.

NATIONAL GUIDE FOR TRAINING PROGRAM

- Urban institutions reported the highest participation rate (42 percent) in National Guide for Training Program. Only 13 percent of the suburban institutions reported participation in this program.

APPRENTICESHIP TRAINING PROGRAM

- Over half of all responding institutions reported participation in the apprenticeship training program. The highest participation rate (63

17

percent) was among suburban institutions and the lowest (48 percent) was among urban institutions.

NONAPPRENTICESHIP INDUSTRY TRAINING

- Nearly 57 percent of the institutions reported participation in the nonapprenticeship training program. Institutions located in rural areas had a significantly higher participation rate (80 percent) than those located in urban and suburban areas.

MILITARY TRAINING

- More than two-thirds (69 percent) of all institutions reported participation in training military personnel. Of these, rural institutions had the highest percentage rate (83 percent). Urban colleges reported a 77 percent rate and suburban colleges a 53 percent rate.

MAXIMUM CREDITS FOR WORK-RELATED EXPERIENCE

The institutions participating in work-related training programs were asked to list the maximum number of credits they awarded to students. Eight out of 10 institutions reported offering between 1 and 20 credits for work-related experience (Table 15).

TABLE 15
AWARDED CREDITS FOR WORK-RELATED EXPERIENCE
BY LOCATION (IN PERCENT)

NUMBER OF CREDITS	URBAN	SUBURBAN	RURAL	TOTAL
1–10	35.7	50.0	40.0	42.9
11–20	35.7	37.5	40.0	37.1
21–30	-	-	-	-
31–40	21.4	-	20.0	11.4
41–50	7.1	12.5	-	8.6
TOTAL	40.0	45.7	14.3	100.0
NO. OF RESPONSES	14	16	5	35

One-half of suburban institutions reported offering between 1 and 10 credits for work-related experience—the highest level of the three sectors. Suburban institutions also led the field in the 41–50 credit category for work experience at the 12.5 percent level (Table 15).

It is important to point out that most institutions did not have significant experience with the issue of awarding credit for work-related experiential learning. In most cases, institutions did have a mechanism in place to assess, measure, and award advanced standing credit for work-related or sponsored training. They did not have the capacity to measure the competencies and/or learning that occurred as a result of individual(s) working at particular tasks and transferring that experience into a learning/credit framework.

FIGURE 5
CREDIT FOR WORK-RELATED EXPERIENCE

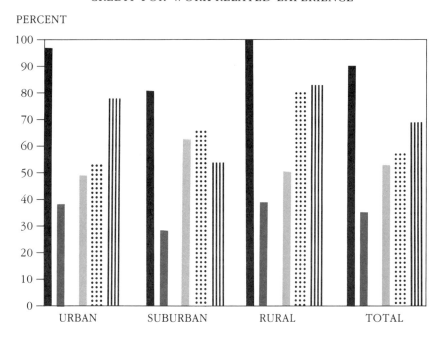

COOP EDUCATION   WORK-STUDY   APPRENTICE TRAINING

NONAPPRENTICE TRAINING   MILITARY

TRANSFER PROGRAMS

Three questions pertained to transfer programs. They were: transfer rate of students to four-year colleges, transfer rate of degree graduates in occupational programs, and the list of transferring institutions.

TRANSFER RATE TO FOUR-YEAR INSTITUTIONS

Nearly 8 out of 10 institutions responded to this item. Of these, over half (52 percent) were urban institutions. Nearly one-third of urban and suburban institutions reported between 1 and 10 percent of their students transferring to four-year institutions, while 17 percent of the rural institutions had this figure (Table 16). One-third of the rural institutions reported a transfer rate of over 50 percent.

TABLE 16

TRANSFER RATE TO FOUR-YEAR COLLEGES BY LOCATION
(IN PERCENT)

PERCENT INTERVAL	URBAN	SUBURBAN	RURAL	TOTAL
1–10	31.8	35.7	16.7	31.0
11–20	18.2	35.7	50.0	28.6
21–30	13.6	14.3	-	11.9
31–40	9.1	14.3	-	9.5
41–50	13.6	-	-	7.1
Over 50	13.6	-	33.3	11.9
TOTAL	52.4	33.3	14.3	100.0
NO. OF RESPONDENTS	22	14	6	42

OCCUPATIONAL PROGRAM GRADUATE TRANSFER

The information on the occupational program graduate transfer rate was scanty and unreliable. Only 22 institutions responded to this question. Of these, 13 were urban, 8 suburban, and 1 rural. The transfer rates listed varied from a low of 1 percent to a high of 50 percent. A majority (two-thirds) fell between 1 and 10 percent (Table 17).

TABLE 17
OCCUPATIONAL PROGRAM GRADUATE TRANSFER BY LOCATION
(IN PERCENT)

PERCENT INTERVAL	URBAN	SUBURBAN	RURAL	TOTAL
1–10	53.9	87.5	100.0	68.2
11–20	23.1	-	-	13.6
21–30	-	-	-	-
31–40	7.7	-	-	4.6
41–50	15.3	12.5	-	13.6
TOTAL	59.1	36.4	4.5	100.0
NO. OF RESPONDENTS	13	8	1	22

TRANSFERRING INSTITUTIONS

A majority of institutions listed the four-year colleges and universities to which their students had transferred. In general, they were in-state, public colleges and universities.

COMMUNITY ECONOMIC PROFILE

In an effort to develop a community economic profile, the institutions were asked to describe the sizes, types, and numbers of industries in which they operate. This data was generally impressionistic on the part of respondents as opposed to hard information. It was the rare college that had a realistic assessment of its economic community. Colleges reported unsuccessful attempts at obtaining this type of information from local governments. It seems many local governments do not collect this data.

The types of industries listed in the survey were heavy and light industries, high technology, service, retail, and others. Over three-fourths of the institutions responded to this part of the survey. Of these, 51 percent represented urban institutions, 39 percent suburban, and 10 percent rural institutions (Table 18).

TABLE 18
ECONOMIC/INDUSTRIAL COMMUNITY
IN WHICH THE COLLEGE OPERATES BY LOCATION
(IN PERCENT)

CATEGORY	URBAN	SUBURBAN	RURAL	TOTAL
Heavy Industry	51.2	39.0	9.8	100.0
Light Industry	52.4	35.7	11.9	100.0
High Technology	52.5	35.0	12.5	100.0
Retail	50.0	38.1	11.9	100.0
Service	100.0	0.0	0.0	100.0
Other	50.0	38.1	11.9	100.0
TOTAL	51.2	40.0	9.8	100.0
NO. OF RESPONDENTS	21	16	4	41

Just over one-half of urban institutions, two-fifths of suburban, and one-tenth of rural institutions reported having heavy, retail, and other industries in their service areas. Fifty-two percent of urban, 36 percent of suburban, and 12 percent of rural institutions reported having light industry and high technology firms. Only urban institutions reported having service-related industries.

It appears that the service areas of urban institutions have a higher concentration of all the above types of industries. In contrast, just over one-third of suburban and one-tenth of rural institutions reported having all but service industries in the areas in which they are located. Regarding the absence of service industries in suburban and rural settings, it is very tempting to speculate that this is a reflection of misunderstanding on the part of the respondents. Intuitively, the expectation is to find some level of service industry in all communities.

HEAVY INDUSTRIES

The institutions were asked to indicate the number of employees engaged in heavy industries and the number of such industries. Nearly 57 percent of all respondents reported that the heavy industries in their areas employed over 3,000 workers (Table 19). Nearly one-third of urban, one-half of suburban, and three-fourths of rural institutions reported less than 3,000 employees in the heavy industries located in their areas.

TABLE 19
NUMBER OF EMPLOYEES IN HEAVY INDUSTRIES BY LOCATION
(IN PERCENT)

NUMBER OF EMPLOYEES	URBAN	SUBURBAN	RURAL	TOTAL
Over 3,000	64.7	56.3	25.0	56.8
2,000–3,000	11.8	12.5	-	10.8
1,000–1,999	5.9	-	50.0	8.1
500–999	11.8	25.0	-	16.2
100–499	5.9	-	-	2.7
Under 50	-	6.3	25.0	5.4
TOTAL	45.9	43.3	10.8	100.0
NO. OF RESPONDENTS	17	16	4	37

TABLE 20
NUMBER OF HEAVY INDUSTRIES BY LOCATION
(IN PERCENT)

NUMBER	URBAN	SUBURBAN	RURAL	TOTAL
Over 20	50.0	37.5	33.3	44.4
10–19	-	12.5	66.7	11.2
5–9	12.5	-	-	7.4
None	25.0	50.0	-	29.6
Other	12.5	-	-	7.4
TOTAL	59.3	29.6	11.1	100.0
NO. OF RESPONDENTS	16	8	3	27

In terms of the number of heavy industries, half of the urban institutions and one-third each of suburban and rural institutions reported over 20 such industries in their service areas (Table 20). In short, the majority of all respondents listed significant concentrations of heavy industries within their service areas.

LIGHT INDUSTRIES

One-half of urban and suburban institutions and one-fifth of rural institutions reported that the light industries located in their areas employed a total of over 3,000 workers (Table 21). Sixty percent of rural institutions had light industries in their areas that employed fewer than 500. In contrast, one-third of urban and one-fifth of suburban institutions reported that the total work force employed by light industries was fewer than 500.

TABLE 21
NUMBER OF EMPLOYEES IN LIGHT INDUSTRIES BY LOCATION
(IN PERCENT)

NUMBER OF EMPLOYEES	URBAN	SUBURBAN	RURAL	TOTAL
Over 3,000	50.0	57.1	20.0	48.7
2,000–3,000	-	7.1	-	2.6
1,000–1,999	5.0	14.3	20.0	10.3
500–999	5.1	-	-	5.1
100–499	24.9	14.3	20.0	17.9
50–99	5.0	7.1	20.0	7.7
Under 50	10.0	-	20.0	7.7
TOTAL	51.3	35.9	12.8	100.0
NO. OF RESPONDENTS	20	14	5	39

TABLE 22
NUMBER OF LIGHT INDUSTRIES BY LOCATION
(IN PERCENT)

NUMBER	URBAN	SUBURBAN	RURAL	TOTAL
Over 20	62.5	100.0	50.0	70.4
10–19	25.0	-		14.8
5–9	-	-	50.0	7.4
1–4	6.3	-	-	3.7
None	6.3	-	-	3.7
TOTAL	59.3	25.9	14.8	100.0
NO. OF RESPONDENTS	16	7	4	27

All suburban, two-thirds of urban, and one-half of rural institutions reported having more than 20 light industries in their service areas (Table 22). As in the case of heavy industry, light industry was well represented in the districts of responding institutions from all geographic areas.

HIGH TECHNOLOGY INDUSTRIES

Nearly two-thirds of urban and one-third of suburban institutions reported the presence of high technology industries employing more than 3,000 (Table 23). All rural institutions reported that the high technology industries in their service districts employed fewer than 500 workers.

TABLE 23
NUMBER OF EMPLOYEES IN HIGH TECH INDUSTRIES BY LOCATION
(IN PERCENT)

NUMBER OF EMPLOYEES	URBAN	SUBURBAN	RURAL	TOTAL
Over 3,000	65.0	33.3	-	45.9
2,000–3,000	-	8.3	-	2.7
1,000–1,999	15.0	25.0	-	16.2
500–999	-	16.7	-	5.4
100–499	5.0	16.7	20.0	10.9
50–99	10.0	-	70.3	13.5
Under 50	5.0	-	7.7	5.4
TOTAL	54.1	32.4	13.5	100.0
NO. OF RESPONDENTS	20	12	5	37

TABLE 24
NUMBER OF HIGH TECH INDUSTRIES BY LOCATION
(IN PERCENT)

NUMBER	URBAN	SUBURBAN	RURAL	TOTAL
Over 20	37.5	50.0	-	35.7
10–19	31.3	-	-	17.9
5–9	-	12.5	-	3.6
1–4	31.3	25.0	100.0	39.3
None	-	12.5	-	3.6
TOTAL	57.1	28.6	14.3	100.0
NO. OF RESPONDENTS	16	8	4	28

One-third of all responding institutions reported having more than 20 high tech industries in their areas (Table 24). All rural institutions reported one to four high technology industries in their areas. One-half of suburban and one-third of urban institutions had more than 20 high tech industries. The data, in this case, support information from other sources that high tech industries are not the nation's dominant economic force.

SERVICE INDUSTRIES

Nearly two-thirds of urban and suburban institutions that responded to the survey reported the existence of service industries that employed a total of over 3,000. A majority (61 percent) of rural institutions reported the existence of such industries with total employment under 100 people (Table 25).

TABLE 25
NUMBER OF EMPLOYEES IN SERVICE INDUSTRIES BY LOCATION
(IN PERCENT)

NUMBER OF EMPLOYEES	URBAN	SUBURBAN	RURAL	TOTAL
Over 3,000	63.6	66.4	-	57.1
2,000–3,000	5.5	-	19.3	5.5
1,000–1,999	5.0	7.1	-	5.1
500–999	5.0	-	-	2.6
100–499	7.0	19.4	20.0	10.9
50–99	7.0	-	20.0	7.7
Under 50	7.0	7.1	40.7	11.1
TOTAL	51.3	35.9	12.8	100.0
NO. OF RESPONDENTS	20	14	5	39

Like high tech industries, service industries reflect the results of other studies. The nation is rapidly increasing the number of service industries in urban, suburban, and rural settings. This study shows that the only major difference in setting is the size of the industry. Rural locations will have fewer service industries with fewer employees (Table 26).

TABLE 26
NUMBER OF SERVICE INDUSTRIES BY LOCATION
(IN PERCENT)

NUMBER	URBAN	SUBURBAN	RURAL	TOTAL
Over 20	81.8	66.7	33.3	70.0
10–19	9.1	16.7	-	10.0
5–9	-	-	66.7	10.0
1–4	-	16.7	-	5.0
None	9.1	-	-	5.0
TOTAL	55.0	30.0	15.0	100.0
NO. OF RESPONDENTS	11	6	3	20

RETAIL INDUSTRIES

Retail industries with more than 3,000 employees were located near a majority (57 percent) of urban and suburban institutions that responded to the survey (Table 27). Eighty percent of rural institutions reported their area retail industries employed fewer than 500 workers.

TABLE 27
NUMBER OF EMPLOYEES IN RETAIL INDUSTRIES BY LOCATION
(IN PERCENT)

NUMBER OF EMPLOYEES	URBAN	SUBURBAN	RURAL	TOTAL
Over 3,000	57.1	57.1	20.0	52.5
2,000–2,999	-	-	-	-
1,000–1,999	9.5	14.3	-	10.0
500–999	9.5	14.3	-	10.0
100–499	9.5	-	60.0	12.5
50–99	-	7.1	-	2.5
Under 50	14.3	7.1	20.0	12.5
TOTAL	52.5	35.0	12.5	100.0
NO. OF RESPONDENTS	21	14	5	40

Over three-fourths of all urban and suburban institutions reported that more than 20 retail industries were located in their service areas (Table 28). Among the rural industries, 60 percent reported having over 20 retail industries and the remaining (40 percent) reported between 5 and 9 such industries in their areas.

TABLE 28
NUMBER OF RETAIL INDUSTRIES BY LOCATION
(IN PERCENT)

NUMBER	URBAN	SUBURBAN	RURAL	TOTAL
Over 20	75.0	77.8	60.0	73.3
10–19	6.3	-	-	3.3
5–9	12.5	11.1	40.0	16.7
1–4	6.3	11.1	-	6.7
TOTAL	53.3	30.0	16.7	100.0
NO. OF RESPONDENTS	16	9	5	30

OTHER INDUSTRIES

Over one-half of all urban and suburban institutions reported other industries in their service areas employing a total of over 3,000 people (Table 29). Eight out of 10 rural institutions reported the existence of other industries that employed a total of fewer than 500 persons.

TABLE 29
NUMBER OF EMPLOYEES IN OTHER INDUSTRIES BY LOCATION
(IN PERCENT)

NUMBER OF EMPLOYEES	URBAN	SUBURBAN	RURAL	TOTAL
Over 3,000	60.0	50.0	20.0	51.3
2,000–3,000	-	7.1	-	2.6
1,000–1,999	5.0	7.1	-	5.1
500–999	5.0	-	-	2.6
100–499	10.0	28.6	20.0	17.9
50–99	10.0	-	20.0	7.7
Under 50	10.0	7.1	40.0	12.8
TOTAL	51.3	35.9	12.8	100.0
NO. OF RESPONDENTS	20	14	5	39

Nearly 90 percent of the urban and suburban institutions reported the presence of more than 20 other industries in their localities. Rural institutions indicated that the rate of "other industry" incidence for the over-20 category was 60 percent (Table 30).

29

TABLE 30
NUMBER OF OTHER INDUSTRIES BY LOCATION
(IN PERCENT)

NUMBER	URBAN	SUBURBAN	RURAL	TOTAL
Over 20	88.2	90.0	60.0	84.4
10–19	-	10.0	20.0	6.3
5–9	5.9	-	20.0	6.3
1–4	5.9	-	-	3.0
TOTAL	53.3	31.3	15.6	100.0
NO. OF RESPONDENTS	17	10	5	32

VII

CORPORATE ORGANIZATIONAL PROFILE

More than half of all urban institutions that responded to the inventory reported that the industries located in their areas were international in scope (Table 31). Just under one-third of the suburban institutions reported their service area industries were international. Only 13 percent of the rural colleges said their local industries were international in scope. The same proportional distribution holds true for national and regionally based corporations. Seventy-one percent of the urban institutions said their local industries were subsidiaries of national or regional firms, while 24 percent of the suburban and 6 percent of the rural institutions reported that their industries did business beyond their immediate geographical areas.

TABLE 31

CORPORATE ORGANIZATIONAL PROFILE BY LOCATION
(IN PERCENT)

OWNERSHIP	URBAN	SUBURBAN	RURAL	TOTAL
International	56.3	31.3	12.5	100.0
National	52.6	36.8	10.5	100.0
Regionally Based Corp.	52.0	36.0	12.0	100.0
Subsidiary	70.6	23.5	5.9	100.0
Other	60.0	40.0	-	100.0
TOTAL	52.0	36.0	12.0	100.0
NO. OF RESPONDENTS	13	9	3	25

MILITARY CONTRACTS

Fewer than half (42 percent) of the institutions reported that they provided formal educational training programs for military personnel (Table 32). Fifty-eight percent of the responding urban institutions said they were engaged in formal educational training for service personnel. In contrast, 30 percent of suburban institutions and 17 percent of rural institutions had engaged in such training activities.

TABLE 32
FORMAL EDUCATION TRAINING FOR MILITARY SERVICE PERSONNEL
BY LOCATION (IN PERCENT)

TRAINING	URBAN	SUBURBAN	RURAL	TOTAL
Yes	58.3	30.0	16.7	42.0
No	41.7	70.0	83.3	88.0
TOTAL	48.0	40.0	12.0	100.0
NO. OF RESPONDENTS	24	20	6	50

SIZE OF MILITARY CONTRACT

The institutions participating in the educational training programs for military personnel were asked to indicate the dollar value of contracts with the military. Only 11 urban and 2 suburban institutions responded to this item (Table 33). The contract amount of urban institutions varied from $2,000 to nearly $950,000, with an average award of $152,000. With respect to the suburban institutions, one received $10,000 and the other, $696,290.

TABLE 33
SIZE OF MILITARY CONTRACT BY LOCATION
(IN PERCENT)

AMOUNT	URBAN	SUBURBAN	RURAL	TOTAL
$ 1,000–9,999	27.3	-	-	23.1
10,000–19,999	-	50.0	-	7.7
20,000–49,999	18.1	-	-	15.4
50,000–99,999	27.3	-	-	23.1
100,000–199,000	9.1	-	-	7.7
200,000–499,999	9.1	-	-	7.7
500,000–999,999	9.1	50.0	-	15.4
TOTAL	84.6	15.4	-	100.0
NO. OF RESPONDENTS	11	2	-	13

Nearly three-fourths of all urban institutions had military contracts ranging from $10,000 to $1 million. One institution had received a contract from the military of nearly $1 million. The stated value of these military contracts indicates that viable training/education relationships do exist between the colleges and the military.

BUSINESS/INDUSTRY/COLLEGE
COLLABORATION

The colleges were asked to furnish information on industries operating within their service areas with which they had a collaborative arrangement. Among the data requested were: name of firm, number of employees, employees enrolled in job-related courses, nature of training support, number of courses offered, source of equipment and instructional materials used in the training program, instructors used in the courses, credits applicability, training involving JTPA, number of programs offered, and funding. The response to this section of the survey was uneven. Some institutions provided detailed information on the above items, while others indicated that such information was unavailable. The ability of many institutions to assess, critique, and promote their business/industry activities is critically handicapped by inadequate data collection at the local level.

PARTNERSHIP TRAINING

Thirty-four of the 58 institutions responded to the industry/college partnership training survey. This yielded a response rate of 62 percent. The number of firms involved in such training programs varied from 40 (5 percent) for rural institutions to 530 (69 percent) for urban institutions (Table 34). A total of 737 companies had a collaborative arrangement with the 36 colleges. These colleges were involved in the training of over 28,000 employees who were taking job-related courses. Nearly 50 percent of the urban institutions trained 84 percent of the total number of trained employees reported by all institutions.

TABLE 34
PARTNERSHIP TRAINING BY LOCATION

COLLEGE LOCATION	COLLEGES		FIRMS		EMPLOYEES IN JRC*	
	NO.	%	NO.	%	NO.	%
Rural	4	16.67	40	5.08	1,805	6.38
Suburban	11	30.56	167	25.69	2,939	10.38
Urban	19	52.77	530	69.23	23,562	83.24
TOTAL	34	100.00	737	100.00	28,306	100.00

*Job-Related Courses.

35

TRAINING SUPPORT

Nearly one-half of the urban, half of the suburban institutions, and two-thirds of rural institutions reported that the employees of their companies were fully subsidized by firms when the employees registered in job-related courses (Table 35).

TABLE 35
TRAINING SUPPORT BY COMPANIES BY LOCATION
(IN PERCENT)

COLLEGE LOCATION	FULL FUNDING	PARTIAL FUNDING	JTPA* FUNDING	NO SUBSIDY	TOTAL NO.	TOTAL %
Rural	60.0	20.0	10.0	10.0	10	100.00
Suburban	50.0	41.7	0.0	8.3	12	100.00
Urban	46.0	37.5	9.4	6.2	32	100.00
TOTAL	50.0	35.2	5.6	9.2	-	100.0
NO. OF RESPONDENTS	27	19	3	5	54	

*Job Training Partnership Act.

Three institutions (2 urban and 1 suburban) reported no subsidy provided for the employees either by the companies or JTPA.

WORK-RELEASE TIME FOR EMPLOYEES TAKING COURSES

Over half of all institutions reported that students from collaborating companies received work-release time (Table 36). Among rural institutions, 67 percent said their students were granted work-release time. Sixty percent of the urban institutions and 45 percent of the suburban institutions reported that employees/students received work-release time for their coursework.

TABLE 36
WORK-RELEASE TIME FOR EMPLOYEES TAKING COURSES
BY LOCATION (IN PERCENT)

COLLEGE LOCATION	WORK-RELEASE TIME PROVIDED NUMBER	%	WORK-RELEASE TIME NOT PROVIDED NUMBER	%	TOTAL NUMBER	%
Rural	6	66.7	3	33.3	9	100.0
Suburban	4	44.5	5	55.5	9	100.0
Urban	15	60.0	10	40.0	25	100.0
TOTAL	25	58.1	18	41.9	43	100.0

COMPANY RECRUITERS ON CAMPUS

The institutions were asked if the company's recruiters had regular interview schedules on their campuses. Among the 16 urban institutions, 7 (44 percent) reported company recruiters having regular interview schedules on their campuses (Table 37). Forty-four percent of rural and 57 percent of suburban institutions reported having recruiters on their campuses.

TABLE 37
COMPANY RECRUITERS HOLDING INTERVIEWS ON CAMPUS
(IN PERCENT)

COLLEGE LOCATION	RECRUITERS HOLDING REGULAR INTERVIEWS ON CAMPUS		RECRUITERS NOT HOLDING REGULAR INTERVIEWS ON CAMPUS		TOTAL	
	NUMBER	%	NUMBER	%	NUMBER	%
Rural	4	44.4	5	55.6	9	100.0
Suburban	4	57.1	3	42.9	7	100.0
Urban	7	43.8	9	56.2	16	100.0
TOTAL	15	46.9	17	53.1	32	100.0

These data reflect a different aspect of the college/employer relationship. The information suggests that many employers look beyond their immediate customized training needs to the baseline education of new employees. In this sense, the college is performing its traditional pre-employment educational role. One could anticipate that many two-year career curricula are tailored to the local economy and that each curriculum was built with the support of local business/industry advisory councils. The advantage of enhancing the collaboration at both pre- and post-employment levels is that instruction can be mutually reinforcing. Under such circumstances, pre-employment education can benefit from constant employer feedback so that curricula remain current.

COURSE/INSTRUCTIONAL PROFILE

NUMBER OF COURSES OFFERED AND COURSE LOCATION

Over 1,000 different courses/programs were offered by the responding institutions to the employees of their area industries. The question was asked in such a way that it was clear from the responses that the course offerings were industry driven. Urban institutions offered a majority (72 percent) of these courses followed by suburban (22 percent) and rural institutions (6 percent).

The institutions also were asked to indicate the location where the courses were offered for the employees. A majority of courses were evenly spread between the plant and the college campus. A small number of courses was offered at other locations. It appears that the classroom follows the student and, according to this data, the plant site is at parity with the campus. Moreover, when in-plant is collapsed with other sites, the campus comes in second (Table 38).

TABLE 38
NUMBER OF COURSES OFFERED AND COURSE LOCATION

| COLLEGE LOCATION | COURSE TITLES | | LOCATION | | | TOTAL | |
	NO.	%	PLANT %	CAMPUS %	OTHER %	NO.	%
Rural	60	6.1	46.1	46.1	7.8	13	100.0
Suburban	218	22.3	45.0	35.0	20.0	20	100.0
Urban	699	71.6	46.4	42.9	10.7	28	100.0
TOTAL	977	100.0	45.9	41.0	13.1	-	100.0

SOURCE OF EQUIPMENT AND INSTRUCTIONAL MATERIAL USED FOR TRAINING

The institutions were asked to indicate the sources of equipment and instructional materials used for technical programs. Over half of the rural institutions reported using company equipment (Table 39). Company equipment was used by 45 percent of suburban and 39 percent of urban institutions. Data reveal that the "other" equipment source category becomes a factor in urban settings (15.4 percent) and suburban settings (11.11 percent). "Other" sources are in evidence at all settings for instructional material, although to a lesser degree in rural settings.

FIGURE 6
BUSINESS/INDUSTRY TRAINING
NUMBER OF DIFFERENT COURSES OFFERED

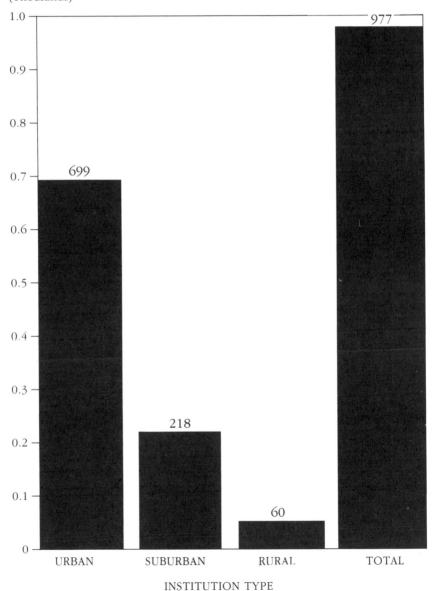

NUMBER OF COURSES
(Thousands)

INSTITUTION TYPE

FIGURE 7
BUSINESS/INDUSTRY TRAINING
LOCATION OF COURSES OFFERED

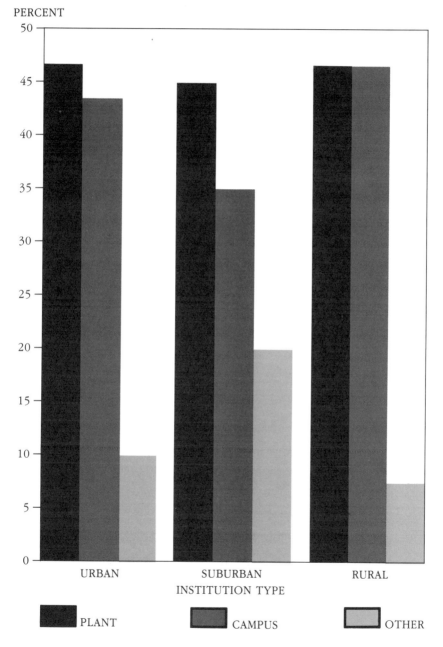

PERCENT

INSTITUTION TYPE

■ PLANT ■ CAMPUS □ OTHER

TABLE 39
SOURCE OF EQUIPMENT AND INSTRUCTIONAL MATERIALS USED FOR TRAINING BY LOCATION
(IN PERCENT)

| COLLEGE LOCATION | EQUIPMENT SOURCE | | | | | INSTRUCTIONAL MATERIALS SOURCE | | | | | |
	COMPANY (%)	COLLEGE (%)	OTHER (%)	TOTAL NO.	TOTAL %	COMPANY %	COLLEGE %	OTHER %	TOTAL NO.	TOTAL %
Rural	54.5	45.5	00.0	11	100.0	41.7	50.0	8.3	12	100.0
Suburban	44.5	44.5	11.0	18	100.0	35.0	40.0	25.0	20	100.0
Urban	38.5	46.1	15.4	26	100.0	26.1	60.9	13.0	23	100.0
TOTAL	43.6	45.5	10.9	-	100.0	32.7	50.9	16.4	-	100.0
NO. OF RESPONDENTS	24	25	6	55		18	28	9	55	

With respect to the source of instructional materials used in the classes, 61 percent of the urban institutions, 40 percent of suburban, and 50 percent of rural institutions used the materials developed at their campuses (Table 39).

These data continue to support the notion that rural colleges develop a substantial symbiotic relationship with their local employers. Whether we are addressing equipment or materials, the rural company is more likely to be a partner on equal footing in the education and training of the local work force. Alternately, this relationship diminishes in suburban and then urban sites.

What also is evident from the data is that in urban and suburban sites the shortfall in company contribution is donated by sources other than the college. The point is that the education/training being delivered is sufficiently expensive that colleges seek a third partner to defray costs of equipment and/or materials. A future study might seek to find out the identity of the third partner.

USE OF INSTRUCTORS

The institutions were asked if the college faculty or company personnel were used to teach the courses. Nearly one-third of all the institutions reported using their own faculty to teach the courses (Table 40). Just over one-fourth of each of the rural (27 percent) and suburban (27 percent) institutions reported using company personnel. One-fifth of the urban institutions reported using company personnel. Nearly one-third of all institutions reported using part-time noncompany faculty to teach the courses.

TABLE 40
INSTRUCTORS USED IN COURSE BY LOCATION
(IN PERCENT)

COLLEGE LOCATION	REGULAR FACULTY	COMPANY PERSONNEL	PART-TIME NONCOMPANY FACULTY	OTHER	TOTAL*	
					NO.	%
Rural	40.0	26.7	26.7	6.6	15	100.0
Suburban	30.8	26.9	34.6	7.6	26	100.0
Urban	31.4	20.0	34.3	14.3	35	100.0
TOTAL	32.9	23.7	32.9	10.5	-	100.0
NO. OF RESPONDENTS	25	18	25	8	76	

*Multiple responses.

Urban institutions lead the other types of institutional categories in providing the requirements of education and training delivery. Urban institutions apparently require less collaborative support from employers as a requisite to providing services. This observation also applies to faculty. Alternately, rural and suburban institutions seek company personnel for instructional purposes at about equal rates.

OFFERING OF COLLEGE CREDITS AND THEIR APPLICABILITY TOWARD AA DEGREE

Over half of all the urban and suburban institutions reported offering college credits for the courses taken by employees (Table 41). Forty-three percent of the rural institutions reported offering college credits for the courses taken by the students.

When the colleges were asked if the credits could be applied toward associate of arts degrees or certificates, three-fourths of all urban and two-thirds of all suburban institutions reported accepting these credits toward either an AA or a certificate. Fifty-five percent of the rural institutions reported the applicability of credits to other than AA degree or a certificate.

TABLE 41
OFFERING OF COLLEGE CREDITS AND THEIR APPLICABILITY
TOWARD AA DEGREE OR CERTIFICATE BY LOCATION
(IN PERCENT)

	COLLEGE CREDITS OFFERED		TOTAL*		CREDITS APPLICABILITY			TOTAL	
	YES	NO	NO.	%	AA DEGREE	CERTIFICATE	OTHER	NO.	%
Rural	42.9	57.1	7	100.0	22.2	22.2	55.6	9	100.0
Suburban	57.1	42.9	14	100.0	41.2	35.3	23.5	17	100.0
Urban	51.9	48.1	27	100.0	37.5	33.3	29.2	24	100.0
TOTAL	52.1	47.9	–	100.0	38.0	32.0	30.0	–	100.0
NO. OF									
RESPONDENTS	25	23	48		19	16	15	50	

*Multiple responses.

COLLEGE CREDITS OFFERED TO COURSES

The study indicates that of the 875 courses (duplicate), 498 (57 percent) were checked *Yes* and 377 (43 percent) were checked *No,* when asked if college credits were given to those courses.

A note of caution!

The information is misleading. Most of the courses/programs are offered under the Continuing Education Unit. This leads the researcher to think that the students might have received CEUs rather than academic credits.

TRAINING INVOLVING JTPA FUNDING

JTPA PARTICIPATING COLLEGES AND NUMBER OF PROGRAMS

The colleges were asked to list the JTPA programs they had offered. Thirty-five of the 58 institutions responded to this item, yielding a 60 percent response rate. Among these colleges, 18 (52 percent) were urban, 12 (34 percent) were suburban, and 5 (14 percent) were rural (Table 42). These institutions reported offering a total of 232 JTPA-sponsored programs. In a breakdown of JTPA programs, nearly 61 percent of the instruction resided in urban institutions, 25 percent in suburban institutions, and 14 percent in rural institutions. Clearly, JTPA-driven instruction is attached to the population centers that are likely to have large numbers of individuals in need of retraining services.

TABLE 42
TRAINING INVOLVING JTPA-PARTICIPATING COLLEGES
AND NUMBER OF PROGRAMS BY LOCATION
(IN PERCENT)

COLLEGE LOCATION	COLLEGES		JTPA PROGRAMS	
	NO.	%	NO.	%
Rural	5	14.29	32	13.79
Suburban	12	34.29	58	25.00
Urban	18	51.42	142	61.21
TOTAL	35	100.00	232	100.00

TRAINING INVOLVING JTPA AND OTHER FUNDING

The institutions were asked to list the number of participants and the amount of JTPA and other funding received for the training programs. According to the survey, a total of nearly 20,000 people participated in the training programs. An overwhelming majority (96 percent) of these participants attended urban and suburban institutions (Table 43).

Total support for the training programs was over $14 million. About three-fourths of this amount came from JTPA. Almost all of this was shared by urban and suburban institutions. Rural institutions shared only 8 percent of the total funding for the training programs. Again, the number of individuals served and dollars involved parallel the data on programs offered. Essentially, urban and suburban institutions in this study are substantially involved with JTPA-funded training. (Note: 30 percent of the respondents did not answer this question. It cannot be determined if this

TABLE 43

TRAINING INVOLVING JTPA AND OTHER FUNDING
(IN PERCENT)

COLLEGE LOCATION	PARTICIPANTS		JTPA FUNDING		OTHER FUNDING		TOTAL	
	NO.	%	AMOUNT	%	AMOUNT	%	AMOUNT	%
Rural	742	3.76	$154,597	1.48	$1,078,764	26.98	$1,233,361	8.52
Suburban	5,999	30.41	4,487,327	42.85	1,922,069	48.08	6,409,396	44.29
Urban	12,989	65.83	5,830,072	55.67	997,278	24.94	6,827,350	47.19
TOTAL	19,730	100.00	$10,471,996	100.00	$3,998,111	100.00	$14,470,107	100.00
PERCENT	–	100.00	–	72.37	–	26.45	–	100.00

lack of response is indicative of an information gap or if it is indicative of no JTPA involvement whatsoever.)

Another comparison in this area is the differential between urban and suburban institutional program costs and individuals served. The data indicate suburban institutions are receiving more than twice as much "other funding" to serve approximately 7,000 fewer participants. The public contribution in this equation remains about equal. The "other" category consisted of a collapsing of state, local, company, and miscellaneous sources.

INVENTORY ANALYSIS

The data developed from this selected inventory of community, technical, and junior colleges reveal some interesting trends in urban, suburban, and rural settings. In some cases, the comparisons within and among settings are rather dramatic. However, the reader must constantly keep in mind that the number of inventory respondents, as well as the original target population, is quite small. Hence, generalizing from this data to the entire system of colleges is risky. On the other hand, many colleges chosen to be in the inventory were from bellwether states and localities that have been very active traditionally in employee education/training. Thus, the trends should not be discounted.

Perhaps the most disturbing result of this inventory is the unevenness of data collection activities from the responding institutions. Clearly, the inventory itself was a difficult instrument in that the desired information had to come from a variety of institutional sources. Even so, the reply to many inventory questions was that the data was nonexistent or too difficult to obtain. For example, only 30 of the 54 institutions replied to the category of questions on JTPA activities. These activities require minimal accounting. In some cases, institutions stated they were too busy delivering services to be bothered with documentation. Alternately, some institutions went to great lengths to comply with inventory requests. Yet even in some other cases, the data was unavailable. Several institutions went the extra mile by trying to acquire community economic profiles from their local governments only to find that these data were not collected.

The primary concern raised by this range of data collection performance is the inability of the colleges to clearly describe their achievements in the area of employee training and education. The data are apparently there, but not in a tangible form to project a global impact statement. Of greatest concern is the proposition that many colleges and, apparently, some local governments do not have a handle on the important components of the local economy. The lack of such data severely hamstrings any type of comprehensive local economic development activity.

Another case in point with respect to weak data is the information collected on part-time/full-time students, occupational course enrollment, and part-time employment. Only 16 institutions could retrieve employment data on their student bodies. This is a critical gap as seen from the little data that are available. Approximately 66.9 percent of the total enrollment is part-time and 33.1 percent of the total is full-time. Therefore, the employment data on part-time students (full-time employees) should provide fundamental information to college policymakers with respect to future initiatives and the likely sources of community support. The results of this inventory suggest that many college officials have not placed any importance on the collection of such data.

This lack of data collection provides the reader with two observations. First, this inventory has uncovered a significant problem in spite of the small target population. The colleges are not routinely collecting data on the employer community, on the occupational background of students, or the specifics of college services delivered to the employer community. The uneven nature of the available data means that generalizations based on this inventory must be handled with great care. On the other hand, the available inventory data does have the impact of stimulating the need for further inquiry in certain areas. The following data analysis also should encourage policymakers to investigate the status of their own institutions on some of these questions.

Urban and suburban institutions are comparable in number of employed students (61–70 percent), while the rural colleges enroll employed students at the 41–50 percent rate. Urban and suburban part-time employment figures are roughly equal (41–50 percent), while the rural figure is 51–60 percent. Full-time employment reveals a figure of 31–40 percent for rural colleges and 41–50 percent for suburban institutions, while urban figures jump to 61–70 percent. The importance of these figures is that they indicate that one-half of the two-year college students in respondent institutions are dividing their attention between work and academics.

However, the figure that captures attention is the urban full-time work category (61–70 percent) that matches the urban part-time enrollment (61–70 percent). All of these figures, but particularly the urban percentages, may presage a major shift in the whole student culture for two-year institutions. These data seem to indicate that two-year colleges are very involved in the education and training (credit level) of working America. The time may be quickly passing when community colleges can be viewed as other postsecondary institutions—primarily serving the traditional (18–20-year-old) student body. The data indicate that urban colleges have, indeed, passed that point and suburban institutions appear to be not far behind. These data confirm information from a variety of sources that indicate that about 75 percent of all credit students are employed. In both cases, two-year colleges are becoming an important pathway to career mobility.

Looking at the data from a different perspective lends strength to other data sources that suggest that two-year institutions are in the midst of a metamorphosis. Inventory information on student age distribution reveals that only one-third of all credit students were under 21 years of age. The average age was 29 urban, 28 suburban, and 27 rural. Over half of these students were between the ages of 22 and 40 years.

The results of these data in urban and suburban settings have some important ramifications for policymakers in academia, corporate offices, and state and federal agencies. Increasingly, the two-year college is becom-

Age Interval	Percentage Total for all settings
22–25	24.1
26–30	20.9
31–40	22.5

ing the educational institution of choice for the 22–40-year-old—the age bracket that is most upwardly mobile in their occupations. These are not the traditional 18–22-year-old college students of 15–20 years ago. Hence, the ongoing interdependency of work and education has become more pronounced at urban and suburban community colleges. That is, in these settings a clear linkage exists between education/training and career/human resource development and the contributions of employees to enrollment stability. Moreover, other data from this study indicate that colleges are increasingly benefiting from the private sector through cash, equipment, and materials donations, and even from contributions to faculty development.

If this trend were to hold true throughout the nation it would leave very few areas in two-year colleges safe from alteration, for what the data reveal is the convergence of two very important trend lines into one that has the likelihood of creating a new synthesis of major importance for the whole nation. We are not just talking about basic changes in a certain stratum of postsecondary institutions to accommodate a new student subgroup. This new student is in the majority, and this student also happens to be the backbone of the economy and the backbone of the tax base. In short, the twin destinies of community colleges and American workers appear to be intertwined in a symbiotic relationship of major proportions. In the words of Dale Parnell, president of the AACJC, "Community colleges could well be on their way to becoming the modern equivalent of the public land grant universities and agricultural extension agencies. They will do for the information age what the land grant universities did for an agricultural and industrial age."

The latter development in American postsecondary education impacted a predominantly agrarian society in such a way as to make the agricultural system of the nation the most productive in the world. The present challenge facing America is the transition from an industrial economy—the challenge of maintaining industrial competitiveness and worker productivity in the face of an equally competitive world economy. The data indicated that community colleges are an increasingly critical component in educating Americans for entry-level occupations. The data also indicate that the colleges are a critical component in an ongoing process of education and training that is necessary for skill maintenance and/or occupational mobility. In short, community colleges appear to be the key educational element in maintaining American economic competitiveness.

Dr. W. Edwards Deming, world-renowned statistical consultant, who after World War II taught the Japanese how to produce high-quality, low-cost products, tells us:

> The community colleges must do it. They are alive to their customers. They are learning how they can help industry in their communities. They must work together because there are a lot of problems that are common to all communities. I believe [the community college] holds the key to teaching American industry what must take place.

Given the significance of such an alignment of destinies, community, technical, and junior colleges may find it useful to rethink the appropriateness of many of their structures for serving the "information age" needs of employees and employers. For example, the emergence of the older student must raise large questions about the very life cycle and basic operations of the college. Has the Carnegie unit of credit measurement become obsolete for a student body reflecting varying levels of advanced educational and skills development? How and where do college administrators schedule classes to meet the educational needs of the dominant student group? More importantly, who pays for employee training—the student, the state, the employer, or some combination of the three? What is the role of financial aid in employee education/training? Does the federal government have a stake in the overall competence of a trained work force? If so, what are the appropriate roles from the Departments of Labor, Commerce, and Education in facilitating national policy and programs? In short, there are significant emerging issues that will require close attention from policymakers.

As indicated earlier, community economic profile data were difficult to obtain. Many colleges had very little idea beyond rough estimates as to the texture of their economic community. It was the rare college that was able to identify the major employers of its community let alone employer education training needs. In this sense, many colleges do not appear to have appreciated the notion that they can play a key catalytic role in the economic development of their communities—a role that places a priority on serving the needs of those already present in the economic community. Such a strategy puts a premium on holding on to what you have. Yet, such a strategy cannot be accomplished without a thorough knowledge of what constitutes the local economic community, along with the creation of a needs assessment profile. It was just such a data base that the inventory was attempting to tap. The usefulness of such information can be implied from the results of the inventory.

The rough data submitted by colleges did construct a profile expected in a comparison of rural, urban, and suburban communities. The mass of industry increases with the population. However, all areas seemed to have a mix of employers. It appeared that this mix of employers might be considered a positive attribute in terms of an institutional service strategy. Colleges could use the shopping center approach by allowing large employers to anchor their programs. They could then meld together small employers into various groups based upon common need. Such a strategy could stimulate the needed critical mass for program delivery and it could also maximize the creation and use of faculty, space, materials, and equipment.

Reversing the strategy, a thorough knowledge of the local corporate profile could be the building block for a community college consortia approach to training/education for national/international companies. Colleges with similar programmatic strengths and objectives could market themselves collectively as viable training networks to be used by appropriate national and regional companies. The Mid-America Training Network (ten Great Lakes community colleges) and the Gulf Coast Consortia (Texas) are good examples of such a strategy. General Motors, Ford, Campbell's Soup, and Motorola are but a few of the increasing number of national companies that are eager to use community colleges in their training strategies. Urban, suburban, and rural colleges reported the presence in their communities of national/international employers at the 50 percent, 31 percent, and 13 percent levels, respectively. Clearly, the networking potential exists for collaborative training on a large scale across these community-based institutions.

In moving from the realm of potential collaboration to that of actual levels of collaboration the inventory results again displayed a weakness. Only 31 of the 54 institutions responded to questions pertaining to college/industry partnership training. A higher response rate was desirable in order to compare accurately the actual activity level against potential activity level. What the data reveal is a substantial amount of collaboration among all responding institutions. These 31 institutions reported working with 650 firms covering 25,096 affected employees. However, the bulk of the work was being done in the urban setting (450 firms—20,804 employees). The surprise was that the suburban activity rate was not nearly as robust (167 firms—2,934 employees). In contrast, the rural respondents only served 33 firms, but those firms accounted for 1,353 employees.

What is striking is the comparison of reported suburban activity level with the suburban economic profile. Notwithstanding the data flaws in the community economic profile, the suburban institutions appear to be operating much below the market capacity of their service areas. Collectively, suburban institutions reported the existence of economic activity that was comparable to urban sites. For example, suburban/urban comparisons on *the number of employees for heavy and light industries* tell an interesting story.

In terms of the presence of employees in the high tech, service, and retail industries, the suburban institutions, with one major exception, report the highest levels of employees within their service area. (The exception is high tech industries with over 3,000 employees.) In short, the suburban institutions appear to have substantial growth capacity in the area of contracted employee education and training.

Employees in Heavy Industry (Percentages)		
	Urban	Suburban
Over 3,000	64.7	56.3
2,000–3,000	11.8	12.5
500–999	11.8	25.0

Employees in Light Industry (Percentages)		
	Urban	Suburban
Over 3,000	50.0	57.1
1,000–1,999	5.0	14.3
100–499	20.0	14.3

The promise woven into such collaboration is apparent through the data involving training support, work release time, instructional site, faculty, and equipment use. This information reflects a pattern of college/employer relationships that are increasingly symbiotic. First, the importance of training and education to employers is underscored by the indicated financial commitments in the inventory. Full subsidization of job-related instruction by employers was reported at the following levels: urban 48.0 percent, suburban 50.0 percent, and rural 62.5 percent. These data imply that training subsidization is well on its way to becoming a formalized strategy to induce employee development. It is noteworthy that the rural colleges in the study benefited at a higher rate than other sites. This may indicate a greater employer reliance on two-year colleges in rural areas.

Easily obscured in this particular data is what appears to be an emerging new consensus on employee (post-service) training as the prime responsibility of the employer. It is in the employer's best interest to maintain a well-trained work force; therefore, it is the employer's responsibility to pay the cost inherent in such an investment. However, this burden is considerably lessened when employers collaborate with public colleges. The full costs of subsidization are reduced with the contribution of public dollars. Increasingly, employee education and training is demanding an employer commitment to a "life-long learning" model in order to maintain competitiveness. With the downturn in traditional student populations, these changes seem to create an optimal climate for the mutual benefit of two-year colleges and employers. The data suggest this scenario is already a strong trend across the nation.

If a future national study substantiated this trend, the implications for decisionmakers could be fundamental. For example, strong national supporting documentation would imply that America has made a de facto commitment to the concept of employee education and training equal to the historical commitment to education and training. For traditional students, given the population demographics and the technologically driven changes in the work force, there is good reason to predict that employee education and training could become the dominant force in two-year colleges. This would mean that, in addition to state dollars, educators and employers alike would have a mutual interest in the status of federal tax credits for employee training. Furthermore, educators might want to give closer scrutiny to their formal structures, which, for the most part, are still shaped to service traditional student populations.

For example, half of the 814 course titles reported in the survey were taught at the plant site for rural, urban, and suburban institutions. When other off-campus sites for employee coursework are added, the campus becomes the preferred site for about a third of the time. Rural colleges are slightly higher on main campus usage. If such coursework represents the wave of the future, then policymakers may want to rethink their campus capital budget. There are other issues and areas to ponder as policymakers begin to fully appreciate the scope of employer/college collaboration.

Again, the data may be a useful glimpse into the future. Over one-half of the employees in the inventory received work-release time. This trend was strongest in urban and rural settings. Acknowledging that we are only talking about five institutions, it is still intriguing to note that work-release time occurred at a 71.4 percent rate in the rural settings. Subsidization and work-release time are substantive comments from those few employers regarding the importance of human resource development to their operations.

Additional data reinforce this viewpoint. Respondents indicated that employers were a major source for instructional equipment and instructional material. Again, the rural institutions appeared to reflect the highest degree of collaboration.

	Equipment Source (percent)			Institutional Material Source (percent)		
	Company	Other	College	Company	Other	College
Rural	55.6	00.0	44.4	45.5	9.0	45.5
Suburban	44.5	11.1	44.5	35.0	25.0	40.0
Urban	33.3	22.2	44.5	22.2	16.7	61.1

From the standpoint of equipment, the college contribution is constant through the different sites. However, urban and suburban institutions seem to be better able to find other sources for the provision of equipment. It is not clear what drives the decision to seek "other" equipment sources. Regarding instructional materials, "other sources" remain an important avenue for instructional support. Urban colleges appear to be in a much better position to provide their own instructional materials, but they still seek significant additional support.

Significant private sector contributions also are being felt in the faculty personnel area. Company personnel are used as faculty 25 percent of the time by rural and suburban colleges. Even the urban colleges use private sector instructors for 14.8 percent of their company courses. On the other hand, all institutions reported using part-time noncompany faculty almost equally. This would seem to support a nationwide trend in college staffing to deliver substantial amounts of instruction through part-time faculty. Questions regarding this group remain. For example: Is this population biased in the direction of occupational/vocational education and training as opposed to traditional transfer curricula? If so, how many of these instructors come from the private sector?

There is another area of observation regarding the growth in employer/college collaboration. The respondents indicated significant willingness to fashion degree-generating credits for employee courses. However, the data in this area revealed a significant difference in the way urban and suburban colleges apply credit as contrasted to the rural colleges. The former seem more amenable to granting credit for employee education/training and more amenable to applying that credit to both associate degrees and certificates. This means that the urban and suburban institutions appear to be more active in applying the traditional collegiate legitimizing function to employee instruction. By extension, it also means that urban and suburban institutions, and to a lesser extent rural institutions, are playing a significant role in moving the associate degree/certificate into the work place as requirements for keeping jobs and advancing in them.

The last item to be considered is the college collaboration generated by the JTPA. The overarching impression given by these data is that the responding community colleges (70 percent) are involved in such activity. Clearly, the active institutions in this category are the colleges in the suburban and urban population centers. This is not surprising, but the differential between urban and suburban "institutional program costs" and "individuals served" is intriguing. Suburban institutions received twice as much "other funding" ($1.9 million vs. $997,278) to serve approximately 2,500 fewer participants than their urban counterparts. "Other funding" consisted of collapsing together state, local, company, and miscellaneous categories. Federal dollars received among the institutions in different locations were more in line with one another, but even there the suburban sites received $227,000 more than urban institutions. It would be useful to track these findings in a national study, with thought toward sifting out the "other funding sources" category.

In conclusion, the results of this inventory indicate that responding two-year colleges reflect extremely rich and varied experiences with respect to employee education and training. In that sense, the very strength of these institutions, their community orientation, makes them very difficult to categorize and assess. More importantly, this particular sample of colleges is far too small to risk generalizations for the breadth of the community college field. However, this sample is large enough and contains enough significant institutions to draw attention to some trends and developments. The greatest concern generated from this study is the difficulty in obtaining consistent and qualitative data in this area across institutions. This raises serious questions with respect to a national follow-up. However, the results of this inventory leave no doubt that a follow-up study would be an essential addition to the growing body of literature on college/employer collaborations.

CONCLUSIONS

The present study examined in detail selected community college part-nerships with business/industry. No attempt was made to select a representative collection of two-year colleges. The survey confirms the findings of the previous study (Day, 1985) that the nation's community, technical, and junior colleges are working cooperatively with area business/industries to provide general and specialized training programs for their employees. The training needs of a vast majority of area industries are being met through these colleges. For these institutions, an average of 21 companies in colleges service districts had collaborative arrangements with an institution in one year. The extent of this collaboration is con-firmed by the fact that almost all institutions had established industrial ad-visory committees for their degree programs. Also, the institutions work closely with the industries by providing academic credit to employees par-ticipating in work-related courses. The companies, in turn, strengthen this cooperation by providing subsidies for their employees and offering plant training sites, instructors, equipment, and instructional materials to the institutions to provide training programs.

OBSERVATIONS

According to the study, successful collaborations between community colleges and business/industry exist today. But there are some concerns with respect to the completion of the inventory. At some institutions, there is a lack of accurate data on noncredit students. The colleges need to refine their methodologies for collecting and maintaining information pertaining to business/industry collaboration.

Aside from the above, there are a number of programmatic recommendations related to community college/business/industry collaborations:

1. Data suggest that a large percentage of institutions work with a number of industries that provide work-release time in order to enhance employee participation in college-sponsored programs. It is recommended that colleges that participated in this type of program should develop close working relationships with local industries.

2. The benefits of using company equipment and materials need to be explored further. In urban and suburban institutions, a higher percentage use their own equipment and materials rather than the company's. It appears that rural community colleges are successful in this regard. A higher level of competition from four-year colleges and universities in urban and suburban areas presents an obstacle for equipment donation from the companies. A well-coordinated effort should be put forth to convince companies to share their equipment.

3. Most institutions reported awarding credit for studies completed in work-study, cooperative education, apprenticeship training, and military training programs. In addition to continuing to award credit for these activities, community colleges need to develop a comprehensive plan to mainstream working adults who bring with them a vast portfolio of work-related learning experiences that could be documented and awarded appropriate college credit.

4. The study revealed that a majority of the institutions had established industrial advisory committees for each program. These efforts should be continued and maintained for planning, refining, and accountability purposes.

5. It appears that the heyday of new capital construction for laboratories and instructional classrooms is over. Due to declining enrollments and the resultant availability of laboratories and classrooms, the community colleges should give serious consideration to bringing in employees from industrial sites and providing them appropriate learning experiences.

6. Community colleges need to place strong emphasis on customizing courses and programs for the market rather than simply repackaging existing curricula.

7. Emphasis should be placed on offering courses/programs for both credit and noncredit.

8. The office of business/industry coordinator should be independent of the continuing education unit. In most cases, economic development programs are successful when the coordinator is in direct contact with the college president and when industries recognize that there is a clear and direct institutional contact to accommodate their needs.

9. An integrated student services system should be developed to effectively serve this new emerging population. The services, among other things, should include assessment, advising, counseling, tutoring, family services, and child care.

10. The results show that the female population is emerging as a new work force in business and industry. The women are entering nontraditional career areas. College staff need to reflect this trend in their services. Further, colleges should develop programs and services appropriate to the population. Colleges should, at the same time, work closely with their employer community to prepare them for entering all phases of the job market.

11. Faculty-industrial exchange programs should be developed to enhance and facilitate program development and faculty development opportunities.

REFERENCES

Action in the States Progress Towards Educational Renewal. A Report by the Task Force on Education for Economic Growth. Education Commission of the States, Denver, 1984.

America's Competitive Challenge—The Need for a National Response: The Report in Brief. A Report to the President of the United States from the Business-Higher Education Forum, April 1983.

Beder H., and Darkenwald, G., *Occupational Education for Adults: An Analysis of Institutional Roles and Relationships.* New Brunswick: Center for Adult Development, Rutgers University, 1979.

Bushnell, D., *Cooperation in Vocational Education.* American Association of Community and Junior Colleges and American Vocational Association, Washington, D.C., 1978.

Campbell, D.F., and Faircloth, D.M., "State Models for Economic Development." *Community and Junior College Journal,* 52(7): 18–19, 1982.

Day, P.R., "Developing Customized Programs for Steel and Other Heavy Industries." *Customized Job Training for Business and Industry,* New Directions for Community Colleges, Vol. 48, December 1984.

Day, P.R., *In Search of Community College Partnerships.* American Association of Community and Junior Colleges, Washington, D.C., 1985.

Eskow, Seymour, "Putting America Back to Work: Phase II." *Community and Junior College Journal,* 54(3): 12–14, 1983.

Goldstein, H., *Training and Education by Industry.* National Institute for Work and Learning, Washington, D.C., 1980.

Jackman, M.J.G., and Mahoney, J.R., *Shoulders to the Wheel: Energy-Related College/Business Cooperative Agreements.* American Association of Community and Junior Colleges, Energy Communications Center, Washington, D.C., 1982.

Mahoney, J.R., *Community College Centers for Contracted Programs: A Sequel to Shoulders to the Wheel.* American Association of Community and Junior Colleges, Energy Communications Center, Washington, D.C., 1982.

Mahoney, J.R., *Putting America Back to Work: The Kellogg Leadership Initiative—A Report and Guidebook.* American Association of Community and Junior Colleges, Washington, D.C., 1984.

Newman, Frank, *Higher Education and the American Resurgence.* The Carnegie Foundation for the Advancement of Teaching, Princeton, New Jersey, 1985.

Nie, N.H., Hull, C.H., Jenkins, J.G., Steinbrenner, K., and Brent, D.H., *Statistical Package for the Social Sciences.* (2nd ed.) McGraw-Hill, New York, 1975.

Nie, N.H., and Hull, C.H. *SPSS Update 7–9.* McGraw-Hill, New York, 1981.

"Putting America Back to Work: A Concept Paper." American Association of Community and Junior Colleges, Washington, D.C., pp. 7–8, 1982.

Warmbrod, C.P., "From Fishing Travelers to Power Plants." *Community and Junior College Journal,* 52(7): 12–14, 1982.

APPENDIX A

EXECUTIVE SUMMARY OF *IN SEARCH OF COMMUNITY COLLEGE PARTNERSHIPS*

A national survey of community, technical, and junior colleges, conducted for the American Association of Community and Junior Colleges (AACJC) and the Association of Community College Trustees (ACCT), reveals the nature and extent of partnerships that exist between colleges and two significant community entities: business/industry and high schools. The results of this study provide valuable information that can help determine future program needs and requirements for technical assistance to these organizations.

Out of the 1,219 colleges surveyed, 770 responded, an overall response rate of 63.2 percent. The highlights of the results are given below.

College Characteristics

- Among the respondents, 78 percent represent community/junior colleges; 14 percent technical colleges; and the remaining represent other types of institutions.
- 55 percent of the respondents are located in urban and suburban areas while 45 percent are located in rural areas.
- 56 percent of the colleges reported they are governed by appointed board members and the remaining 47 percent are governed by locally elected members.

Business, Industry, Labor Council (BIC)

- 41 percent of the respondents have established Business, Industry, Labor Councils on their campuses.
- 76 percent of those who said they have established BICs have done so on a formal basis.
- Nearly one-fourth of the colleges house the BICs on their campuses.
- About one-third of the BICs are funded publicly; one-tenth receive both public and private funding, and over one-half have no funding to support their councils.
- About one-half of all the respondents who reported receiving support receive it from federal and state funding sources; corporations support nearly 17 percent of the councils.

Private Industry Council (PIC)

- Two-thirds of all respondents indicated that they participate in the area Private Industry Council.

Business/Industry Coordination

- Two-thirds of the respondents have appointed business/industry coordinators on their campuses.

Large Private Sector Employer Training

- Nearly three-fourths of all respondents said they offer employee training programs for large private sector employers.
- Nearly 41 percent of all respondents offer customized training; 28 percent provide job-specific training, 14 percent offer generic training; and 9 percent provide all three types of training.
- 30 percent of all respondents provide employee training programs for major, local labor unions.
- 78 percent of the respondents reported offering training at plant/business sites.
- 35 percent of the respondents reported contract training as the main source of funding for their cooperative efforts with local business; 31 percent reported income from tuition; 23 percent indicated state grants as a method of supporting these activities; 10 percent of the respondents listed federal grants as a source of support.
- 68 percent of the respondents reported that their training is subsidized by state and/or local funding.
- 26 percent of the respondents provided contract training for the area employment security system.

Public Sector Employers

- Three-fourths of all respondents reported that they offer training for public sector employees. More urban and suburban colleges (80 percent) engage in such training than do institutions located in rural areas (70 percent).
- Nearly one-half of all the public employee training provided by the respondents is for the employees of city and county governments. Training employees of school districts is second (23 percent); 11 percent of the respondents train state government employees.

Small Business Support

- 83 percent of the respondents reported providing small business support beyond traditional credit coursework.

- One-third of all respondents who provide support to small business offer it in the form of short-term workshops/seminars; 23 percent of the respondents offer short courses; 19 percent of the respondents offer technical assistance.
- Nearly two-thirds of all respondents reported offering small business support services in credit form.

High School/College Partnerships

- Nearly nine out of ten respondents said they have collaborative arrangements with the high schools in their areas.
- More than two-thirds of the colleges reported offering credit courses to local high school students; one-tenth offer noncredit courses; and over one-fifth reported offering both credit and noncredit courses to high school students.
- 30 percent of the respondents reported having advanced placement programs; 29 percent have articulated some of their courses with the schools; 13 percent share faculties; 11 percent indicated that they have cooperative program enrollments; and 11 percent reported that they share facilities with local schools.

Economic Development Offices

- 80 percent of the colleges reported involvement with local and state economic development offices.
- 52 percent of all respondents reported cooperative programs with both local and state economic development offices; 34 percent reported such relationships with only local offices; and 14 percent reported involvement with state economic development offices only.
- Nearly one-half of all respondents reported providing technical assistance to economic development offices.

APPENDIX B

DIRECTORY OF RESPONDENTS

COLLEGE NAME	RESPONDENT & TITLE
RURAL	
Bay De Noc Community College Escanaba, MI 49829 (906) 786-5802	James Peterson Dean of Student Services
College of Southern Idaho P.O. Box 1238 Twin Falls, ID 83303-1238 (208) 733-9554	N. Robert Wright, Jr. Director of Admissions & Records
Illinois Central College East Peoria, IL 61635 (309) 694-5436	Dr. Gerald Holzhauer Director of Academic Support Services
Jamestown Community College 525 Falconer Street Jamestown, NY 14701 (716) 655-5220	Rose M. Scott Director of Development Center for Business
North Dakota State School Wahpeton, ND 58075 (701) 671-2249	Alvin C. Eckre Director of Admission Services
Northern Essex Community College 100 Elliott Street Haverhill, MA 01830 (617) 374-0721	Dr. Ann Marie Delaney Research Director
Williamsport Area Community College 1005 W. Third Street Williamsport, PA 17701-9981 (717) 326-3761	Kathryn Marcello Director of Institutional Research

COLLEGE NAME	RESPONDENT

SUBURBAN

Asnuntuk Community College
P.O. Box 68
Enfield, CT 06820
(203) 745-1603

Brian Rivard
Registrar

Catonsville Community College
800 South Rolling Road
Catonsville, MD 21228
(301) 455-4777

P. Michael Carey
Associate Dean–Continuing
  Education, Career Programs &
  Community Services

College of DuPage
22nd Street and Lambert Road
Glen Ellyn, IL 60137
(312) 858-2800

Gary Rice
Director of Research and Planning

Community College of Rhode
  Island
400 East Avenue
Warwick, RI 02886
(401) 825-1000

Richard Anderson
Coordinator of Business/Industry
  Programs

DeKalb Community College
495 N. Indian Creek Drive
Clarkston, GA 30021
(404) 299-4093

Berman E. Johnson
Director of Research & Planning

Delaware Technical &
  Community College
P.O. Box 897
Dover, DE 19903
(302) 736-3732

Anthony Digenakis
Assistant to President for
  Specialized Training

Dundalk Community College
7200 Sollers Point Road
Baltimore, MD 21222
(301) 522-5709

Dr. K. Rajasekhara
Director of Research & Grants

Ft. Steilacoom Community
  College
9404 112th Street East
Puyallup, WA 98373
(206) 848-9331

Martin Lind
Coordinator of Special Projects

COLLEGE NAME	RESPONDENT
Hagerstown Junior College 751 Robinwood Drive Hagerstown, MD 21740 (301) 790-2800	M. Parsons Dean of Instruction
Henry Ford Community College 5101 Evergreen Dearborn, MI 48128 (313) 271-2750	J. Michael Meade
Mt. Hood Community College 26000 SE Stark Gresham, OR 97030 (503) 667-7312	Barbara Updegraff
Macomb Community College 44575 Garfield Road Mount Clemens, MI 48044 (313) 285-2052	Edward F. Breen Director of Research
Middlesex County College Woodbridge Avenue Edison, NJ 08818 (201) 548-6000	Dr. Madan Capoor Director of Research & Planning
Northern Virginia Community College 4001 Wakefield Chapel Road Annandale, VA 22003 (703) 323-3129	Office of Institutional Research
Northampton County Area Community College 3835 Green Pond Road Bethlehem, PA 18017 (215) 861-5456	James G. Kennedy Director of Research & Planning
Orange County Community College 115 South Street Middletown, NY 10940 (914) 343-1121 x1050	Gail Mee Director of Institutional Research

COLLEGE NAME	RESPONDENT
Pima Community College 1225 North 10th Avenue Tucson, AZ 85705 (601) 884-6666	Carl Webb Business/Industry Coordinator
Pitt Community College P.O. Box Drawer 7007 Greenville, NC 27834 (919) 756-3130	Jack Robinson Coordinator of Cooperative Skills
Pueblo Community College 900 W. Orman Avenue Pueblo, CO 81004 (303) 549-3331	Dr. Larry Moorman Dean of Adult & Continuing Education
State Technical Institute at Memphis 5983 Macon Cove Memphis, TN 38134 (901) 377-4235	Cheryl A. Bingham Manager of Special Projects
Westark Community College P.O. Box 3649 Fort Smith, AR 72903 (501) 785-4241	Sandi Sanders Director of Continuing Education

COLLEGE NAME	RESPONDENT
URBAN	
Anchorage Community College 2533 Providence Avenue Anchorage, AK 99508 (907) 786-1654	Dr. Loretta Seppanen Director of Institutional Research
City College of San Francisco 50 Phelan Avenue San Francisco, CA 94112 (415) 239-3000	Larry Broussal Dean, Admissions & Records Shirley Kelly Dean of Instruction

COLLEGE NAME	RESPONDENT
Community College of Allegheny County 800 Allegheny Avenue Pittsburgh, PA 15233 (412) 323-2323	Diana L. Smyrl Director of Training & Economic Development
Community College of Philadelphia 1700 Spring Garden Street Philadelphia, PA 19130 (215) 751-8029	Thomas R. Howks Assistant to President
Community College of Spokane N. 1810 Greene Street Spokane, WA 99203 (509) 459-3779	F. Leigh Hales Assistant Dean, Business/Industry
Central Piedmont Community College P.O. Box 35009 Charlotte, NC 28235 (704) 373-6633	Otto A. Lockee Vice President of Corporate Services
Chicago City-Wide College 420 N. Wabash Avenue Suite 703 Chicago, IL 60611 (312) 670-0436	Sandra Foster Executive Director, Business/Industry
Cuyahoga Community College 700 Carnegie Avenue Cleveland, OH 44115 (216) 348-4776	Institutional Planning & Research
Dallas County Community College District 701 Elm, Suite 200 Dallas, TX 75202 (214) 746-2449	John W. Pruitt Career & Continuing Education Assistance

COLLEGE NAME	RESPONDENT

Eastern Iowa Community
  College
2804 Eastern Avenue
Davenport, IA 52803
(319) 322-5015

Gary Mohr
Eastern Iowa Business/Industry
  Center

El Paso Community College
P.O. Box 20500
El Paso, TX 79998
(915) 534-4038

Dr. Josefina Veloz
Director of Institutional Evaluation

Fashion Institute of Technology
227 West 27th Street
New York, NY 10001
(212) 760-7672

Dr. G. Appignani
Vice President for Development

Florida Junior College
101 West State Street
Jacksonville, FL 32202
(904) 633-8284

Dr. James R. Meyers
Dean of Occupational Education

Honolulu Community College
874 Dillingham Blvd.
Honolulu, HI 96817
(808) 845-9122

Walter P.S. Chun
Director of Special Programs

Kansas City Kansas Community
  College
7250 State Avenue
Kansas City, KS 66212
(913) 334-1100 x165

G.F. Dietrich
Director of Community Education

Maricopa County Community
  College
3910 E. Van Buren
Phoenix, AZ 85034
(602) 267-4473

John Lewis
Coordinator, Business/Industry
  Training Service

Metropolitan Community
  College
3822 Summit Road
Kansas City, MO 64111
(816) 756-0220

Charles F. Henry
Director, High Technology
  Training Resource Center

COLLEGE NAME	RESPONDENT

Metropolitan Technical
  Community College
P.O. Box 3777
Omaha, NE 68103
(402) 449-8417

Henry Wm. Pliske
Director of Coll. Planning &
  Development

Miami-Dade Community College
950 N.W. 20th Street
Miami, FL 33127
(304) 347-4133

William Succop
Dean, Occupational Education

Minneapolis Community College
1501 Hennepin Avenue
Minneapolis, MN 55409
(612) 341-7022

C.M. Heelan
Associate Dean of Instruction

Peralta Community College
  District
333 E. Eighth Street
Oakland, CA 94606
(415) 466-7314

McKinley Williams
Director of Research Planning &
  Development

Portland Community College
12000 S.W. 49th Ave.
Portland, OR 97219
(503) 244-6111

Chris Meyers
Coordinator of Program Marketing

Rancho Santiago Community
  College
17th & Bristol Streets
Santa Ana, CA 92706
(714) 667-3497

Paul Amorino
Coordinator of Occupational
  Education, Spec.

Sinclair Community College
444 W. Third Street
Dayton, OH 45402
(513) 226-2854

Elizabeth Klauk
Director of Institutional Research
  & Information Systems

State Technical Institute at
  Knoxville
P.O. Box 19802
5908 Lyons View Drive
Knoxville, TN 37939-2802
(615) 584-6103

Lonnie Butler
Director of Institutional Research

COLLEGE NAME

RESPONDENT

Valencia Community College
P.O. Box 3028
Orlando, FL 32802
(305) 299-5000

Dr. Thomas J. Ribley
Assistant Vice President for
Institutional Services

APPENDIX C

KEEPING AMERICA WORKING INDUSTRY TRAINING INVENTORY

Please contact James McKenney (202) 293-7050 with any questions regarding the survey.

(Please print.)

I. *GENERAL*
1. Name of college: _____
2. FICE Code No.: _____
3. Name of staff completing this survey: _____
   Title: _____
   Address: _____
   _____
   _____
   Phone: (____) _____

II. *CREDIT ENROLLMENT (Fall 1984)*
5. Number FTE _____ Total headcount _____
6. Percentage (%) of that headcount taking occupational/technical courses _____
7. Enrolled: ____ % Total ____ % Part-time ____ % Full-time
8. Employed: ____ % Total ____ % Part-time ____ % Full-time
9. Sex: ____ % Male ____ % Female
10. Ethnic: ____ % Caucasian ____ % Black
    ____ % Hispanic ____ % Native American
    ____ % Asian ____ % Other
11. Age: ____ % under 21 ____ % 22 to 25
    ____ % 26 to 30 ____ % 31 to 40
    ____ % 41 to 50 ____ % 51 to 60
    ____ % over 60
12. The average age is _____

III. *NONCREDIT ENROLLMENTS (Fall 1984)*
13. Number _____
14. Percent registered in occupational/technical courses _____ %
15. Employed: ____ % Total ____ % Part-time ____ % Full-time
16. Sex: ____ % Male ____ % Female
17. Ethnic: ____ % Caucasian ____ % Black
    ____ % Hispanic ____ % Native American
    ____ % Asian ____ % Other

18. Age: ___ % under 21   ___ % 22 to 25
                  ___ % 26 to 30   ___ % 31 to 40
                  ___ % 41 to 50   ___ % 51 to 60
                  ___ % over 60

19. The average age is _____

IV. *TECHNICAL AND VOCATIONAL PROGRAMS*

20. Number of occupational programs leading to an associate degree: _____
    Number of occupational programs leading to a certificate: ___
    Does each degree program have an Advisory Committee from industry?   ___ yes   ___ no

21. What occupational degree programs enroll the greatest numbers of employees from given firms? List four or five.

Program	Firm
a. _____	a. _____
b. _____	b. _____
c. _____	c. _____
d. _____	d. _____
e. _____	e. _____

22. What formal arrangements does the college make for awarding credit for work-related experience?

    A) Cooperative Education   yes ___   no ___
    B) Work-Study   yes ___   no ___
    C) National Guide for Training Program   yes ___   no ___
       (American Council on Education)
    D) Apprenticeship Program Training   yes ___   no ___
    E) Nonapprenticeship Industry Training   yes ___   no ___
    F) Military Training   yes ___   no ___
    G) Other   yes ___   no ___
       Identify: _____
       _____
       _____

    If the college does offer credit for work-related experience, what is the maximum number of credits that may be obtained? _____

V. *TRANSFER PROGRAMS*

23. List the four institutions to which *most* of the students who are pursuing baccalaureate degrees transfer:
    a. _____
    b. _____
    c. _____
    d. _____

24. Approximately _____ percent of students transferred to 4-year institutions in 1983?

25. Of the total accepted for transfer by 4-year institutions, what number were degree graduates in occupational/technical fields? _____

26. What was the total number of your students transferring to 4-year institutions in 1983, regardless of whether they completed a degree or certificate program with your college? _____

27. Of your current (1984) total student population, how many have completed degree programs already? (If 1984 data are not available, please substitute 1983 numbers.)

Degree	Year
_____Associate Degree	_____
_____Bachelor's Degree	_____
_____Master's Degree	_____
_____PhD Degree	_____

VI. COMMUNITY ECONOMIC PROFILE

Check the characteristics in each column that best describe the economic/industrial community in which your college operates:

____ Heavy Industry
- ____ Over 3,000 Employees   ____ Over 20
- ____ 2,000–3,000 Employees   ____ 10–19
- ____ 1,000–1,999 Employees   ____ 5–9
- ____ 500–999 Employees   ____ 1–4
- ____ 100–499 Employees   ____ None
- ____ 50–99 Employees
- ____ Under 50 Employees

____ Light Industry
- ____ Over 3,000 Employees   ____ Over 20
- ____ 2,000–3,000 Employees   ____ 10–19
- ____ 1,000–1,999 Employees   ____ 5–9
- ____ 500–999 Employees   ____ 1–4
- ____ 100–499 Employees   ____ None
- ____ 50–99 Employees
- ____ Under 50 Employees

____ High Technology
- ____ Over 3,000 Employees   ____ Over 20
- ____ 2,000–3,000 Employees   ____ 10–19
- ____ 1,000–1,999 Employees   ____ 5–9
- ____ 500–999 Employees   ____ 1–4
- ____ 100–499 Employees   ____ None
- ____ 50–99 Employees
- ____ Under 50 Employees

____ Service
- ____ Over 3,000 Employees   ____ Over 20
- ____ 2,000–3,000 Employees   ____ 10–19
- ____ 1,000–1,999 Employees   ____ 5–9
- ____ 500–999 Employees   ____ 1–4
- ____ 100–499 Employees   ____ None
- ____ 50–99 Employees
- ____ Under 50 Employees

____ Retail	____ Over 3,000 Employees	____ Over 20
	____ 2,000–3,000 Employees	____ 10–19
	____ 1,000–1,999 Employees	____ 5–9
	____ 500–999 Employees	____ 1–4
	____ 100–499 Employees	____ None
	____ 50–99 Employees	
	____ Under 50 Employees	
____ Other	____ Over 3,000 Employees	____ Over 20
	____ 2,000–3,000 Employees	____ 10–19
	____ 1,000–1,999 Employees	____ 5–9
	____ 500–999 Employees	____ 1–4
	____ 100–499 Employees	____ None
	____ 50–99 Employees	
	____ Under 50 Employees	

B. ORGANIZATIONAL PROFILE
   1. Independent local ownership
      ____ Regional-based corporate
      ____ Subsidiary
      ____ National
      ____ International
      ____ Etc.
   2. Please list at least 3 of the private companies with which you have ongoing training programs:

   Name of Company   / Average No. of Trainees/Year
   _____ / _____
   _____ / _____
   _____ / _____

C. MILITARY CONTRACTS
   1. Does your college conduct formal educational training for service personnel at any military base(s) located in your service area?   yes ____   no ____   If yes, list base(s):
   _____
   _____
   _____
   _____

   2. The largest military contract for 1984 was valued at
      $ _____ .

Thank you for your assistance. Please return the form to: Dr. K. Rajasekhara, Director of Institutional Research and Grants, Dundalk Community College, 7200 Sollers Point Road, Dundalk, MD 21222

VII. KAW EMPLOYMENT DATA SURVEY

COMPANY: (If company is national or multi-national, give data only for plants and/or operations within your college district. Please give company's full name and the name and titles of both its principal officer (CEO) in your district and the senior executive in charge of training. If you are a multi-campus district, please provide composite data for all your colleges.)

	Number of full-time employees	Total number of employees	Number of employees who hold degrees or occupational certificates from your college	Number of employees currently enrolled in job-related courses in your college	Are the employees taking job-related courses fully or partially subsidized by the company? Check the company: appropriate box.	Does company provide work-release time for employees to take these job-related courses?	Do the company's recruiters have regular interview schedules on your campus?
Firm _____ CEO _____ Training Executive _____ Phone Number _____					___ Fully ___ Partially ___ No subsidy ___ JTPA	___ Yes ___ No	___ Yes ___ No
Firm _____ CEO _____ Training Executive _____ Phone Number _____					___ Fully ___ Partially ___ No subsidy ___ JTPA	___ Yes ___ No	___ Yes ___ No
Firm _____ CEO _____ Training Executive _____ Phone Number _____					___ Fully ___ Partially ___ No subsidy ___ JTPA	___ Yes ___ No	___ Yes ___ No
Firm _____ CEO _____ Training Executive _____ Phone Number _____					___ Fully ___ Partially ___ No subsidy ___ JTPA	___ Yes ___ No	___ Yes ___ No

(a) Duplicate this sheet as many times as necessary to give your complete list of major employers, per instructions.

(b) For each firm you list, please complete the "course list" which is the second page of the survey instrument.

VIII. COURSE LIST

From preceding page: Firm Number (#) _____ . Firm Name _____ .

List for each firm up to ten courses in which the company's employees are most heavily or most frequently enrolled. List them in descending rank of enrollment and provide current estimates of company's employees enrolled in the course, if such estimates are available. Check more than one response if appropriate.

Course Title	Course location (company plant, campus)	Source of equipment (company, college)	Source of instruction materials	Instructors used in course	College credit given	Credit applies toward two-year degree or certificate
1.	— Plant — Campus — Other	— Company — College — Other	— Company — College — Other	— Regular faculty — Co. Personnel — PT non-Co. fac.* — Other	— Yes — No	— Degree — Certificate — Other
2.	— Plant — Campus — Other	— Company — College — Other	— Company — College — Other	— Regular faculty — Co. Personnel — PT non-Co. fac.* — Other	— Yes — No	— Degree — Certificate — Other
3.	— Plant — Campus — Other	— Company — College — Other	— Company — College — Other	— Regular faculty — Co. Personnel — PT non-Co. fac.* — Other	— Yes — No	— Degree — Certificate — Other
4.	— Plant — Campus — Other	— Company — College — Other	— Company — College — Other	— Regular faculty — Co. Personnel — PT non-Co. fac.* — Other	— Yes — No	— Degree — Certificate — Other
5.	— Plant — Campus — Other	— Company — College — Other	— Company — College — Other	— Regular faculty — Co. Personnel — PT non-Co. fac.* — Other	— Yes — No	— Degree — Certificate — Other
6.	— Plant — Campus — Other	— Company — College — Other	— Company — College — Other	— Regular faculty — Co. Personnel — PT non-Co. fac.* — Other	— Yes — No	— Degree — Certificate — Other
7.	— Plant — Campus — Other	— Company — College — Other	— Company — College — Other	— Regular faculty — Co. Personnel — PT non-Co. fac.* — Other	— Yes — No	— Degree — Certificate — Other

* Part-time noncompany faculty

(a) Duplicate this sheet as many times as necessary to make your COURSE LIST for each campus.

IX. TRAINING INVOLVING JTPA FUNDING:

JTPA Program Title	Description	Dates	Budget Total $	Budget JTPA $	State	County	City	Company	Other	Number of Participants	Administrative Entity/Unit
1.											

APPENDIX D

LIST OF UNDUPLICATED COURSES OFFERED
BY PARTICIPATING COLLEGES TO BUSINESS AND INDUSTRY

LOCATION	COLLEGE NAME	COURSE TITLE
RURAL	Bay De Noc Community College Escanaba, MI 49829 (906) 786-5802	1. Basic Industrial Hydraulics 2. Blueprint Reading 3. Electrical 4. Interaction Mgmt. Training 5. Shop Math 6. Welding
	College of Southern Idaho P.O. Box 1238 Twin Falls, ID 83303-1238 (208) 733-9554	1. Accounting 2. Computer-related courses 3. Economics 4. Marketing 5. Supervision
	Jamestown Community College 525 Falconer Street Jamestown, NY 14701 (716) 665-5220	1. Electric Trouble Shooting 2. First-Line Managers 3. Genesis 2000 Training 4. Mig Welding 5. Production Manager Workshop 6. Quality Training 7. Special Woven Workshop 8. Statistical Process Control 9. Supervisory Training Program 10. Three-Phase Sewing Project
	North Dakota State School Wahpeton, ND 58075 (701) 671-2249	1. Computer Programming-BASIC 2. Computer Training 3. Geometric Tolerance 4. Introduction to Computers 5. Plant Maintenance Mechanics 6. Quality Control 7. Welding

LOCATION	COLLEGE NAME	COURSE TITLE

Northern Essex Community College
100 Elliott Street
Haverhill, MA 01820
(617) 374-0721 X199

1. Cardiovascular System
2. Children's Literature
3. Computer Literacy
4. Creative Experience
5. Gastrointestinal System
6. Personal Computers
7. Principles of Materials Mgmt.
8. Problems of Early Child Ed.
9. Respiratory System
10. Speech & Language
11. Statistical Quality Control
12. Tech Writing for Professional

Williamsport Area Community College
1005 W. Third Street
Williamsport, PA 17701-9981
(717) 326-3761

1. A.C. Theory & Applications
2. Arc & Heliarc Welding
3. Auto Air Conditioning
4. Basic Motor Control
5. Basic Sheet Metal Fabrication
6. D.C. Theory & Applications
7. Electric Fundamentals
8. Electric Motor Control
9. Electronics Troubleshooting
10. First-Line Supervision
11. Intro. to Microcomputers
12. Intro. to Word Star
13. Lotus 1-2-3
14. Motor Control -2
15. Statistical Process Control
16. Technical Math
17. Technical Physics I
18. Technical Physics II

TOTAL RURAL   58

SUBUR-BAN

College of DuPage
22nd Street & Lambert Road
Glen Ellyn, IL 60137
(312) 858-2800

1. Accounting for Managers
2. Air Conditioning
3. Allied Health Courses
4. Basic Die Theory
5. Basic Ind. Hydraulics
6. Basic Investment
7. Blueprint Reading
8. Child Care Development
9. Comm. Skills for Managers
10. Computer Basics for Managers

LOCATION	COLLEGE NAME	COURSE TITLE
		11. Computer Literacy
		12. Conventional Printing
		13. Corp. Gamesmanship for Women
		14. Effective Leadership
		15. Effective Listening for Bus.
		16. Electronics Technology
		17. English Courses
		18. Financial Planning for Women
		19. How to Write Winning Reports
		20. Increase Your Supervisory Knowhow
		21. Industrial Physics
		22. Industrial Pipe Fitting
		23. Intro. to Data Processing
		24. Jig and Fixtures
		25. Management by Objectives
		26. Manufacturing Tech.
		27. Mathematics
		28. Medical Radiography
		29. Medical Terminology
		30. Memory Skills
		31. Metals Industry
		32. Microcomputers
		33. Multimedia First Aid
		34. Nurses Aid Training
		35. Patient Ed. Workshop for Nurses
		36. Pediatric Cardio-Pulmon. Assess.
		37. Physical Assess. of Older Adults
		38. Plastic Technology
		39. Principles of Marketing
		40. Sales Skills Seminar
		41. Select Software
		42. Shop Math
		43. Strength Quality Assurance
		44. Success Through Assertive Mgmt.
		45. Telemarketing
		46. Tool Making Theory
		47. Welding
		48. Writing for Mgmt. Success
		49. Writing for Management

LOCATION	COLLEGE NAME	COURSE TITLE

Dundalk Community College
7200 Sollers Point Road
Baltimore, MD 21222
(301) 522-5709

1. Computer Literacy
2. Confined Space Rescue
   Training
3. Electronics
4. Human Relations
5. Industrial Bearing & Seals
6. Industrial Measurements
7. Inspector Planner
8. Intro. Data Processing
9. Labor Relations
10. Leadership Skills
11. Mathematics
12. Mechanical Drive
    Components
13. Pipe Fitting
14. Pump Packing
15. Stress Management
16. Supervisor Practices
17. Time Management
18. Welding
19. Writing Skills

Ft. Steilacoom Community College
9404 112th Street East
Puyallup, WA 98373
(206) 848-9331

1. Active
2. Calculus I
3. Computer Architecture
4. Digital Systems
5. Engine Repair Principles

Mt. Hood Community College
26000 SE Stark
Gresham, OR 97030
(503) 667-7312

1. Basic Arrhythmia
2. Blueprint Reading &
   Sketching
3. COBOL
4. Communications for
   Supervisors
5. Computer Numerical
   Control
6. Customer Relations
7. Drug & Alcohol Abuse
8. Elements of Supervision
9. FORTRAN
10. Fire Science Courses
11. Fundamentals of Speech
12. Hardware Overview
13. Intro. to Business
14. Introduction to Computers
15. Lotus 1-2-3
16. Management Courses
17. Physical Assessment
18. Police Science Courses

LOCATION	COLLEGE NAME	COURSE TITLE
		19. Presentation Skills
		20. Software Overview
		21. Stop Smoking
		22. Stress Management
		23. Written Communication
	Northampton County Area Community College 3835 Green Pond Road Bethlehem, PA 18017 (215) 861-5456	1. Budgeting 2. Comm. Skills for Managers 3. Effective Supervision 4. Fundamentals of Marketing 5. Planning & Control 6. Principles of Finance 7. Secretarial Effectiveness 8. Telephone Techniques 9. Time Management 10. What Managers Do 11. Word Processing
	Orange County Community College 115 South Street Middletown, NY 10940 (914) 343-1121 x1050	1. Blueprint Reading 2. Computer Literacy 3. Computer Training 4. Manufacturing Operator Training 5. Math. Appn. Blueprint Reading 6. Supervisory Training 7. Technical Writing
	Pima Community College 1225 North 10th Ave. Tucson, AZ 85705 (602) 884-6666	1. Accounting 2. Administration of Justice 3. Astronomy 4. Automotive Technology 5. Business 6. Computer Science 7. Drafting 8. Electronics 9. Engineering Construction Tech. 10. Human Development 11. Management 12. Mathematics 13. Microelectronics 14. Psychology 15. Quality Control Certification 16. Solder Training 17. Speech 18. Tire Science 19. Woodshop 20. Writing

LOCATION	COLLEGE NAME	COURSE TITLE

State Technical Institute at
Memphis
5983 Macon Cove
Memphis, TN 38134
(901) 377-4235

1. A.C. Circuits
2. Air Conditioning
3. BASIC Programming for Tech.
4. Basic Math
5. Blueprint Reading
6. Computer Systems
7. D.C. Circuits
8. Electrical Machines & Control
9. Frontline Supervision
10. Human Relations
11. Industrial Electricity
12. Intro. to Electronic Tech.
13. Mechanical Tech Refresher
14. Microcomputer Applications
15. Minicomputer Applications
16. Oral Communications
17. Participative Management
18. Quality Control
19. Solid State Devices

Westark Community College
P.O. Box 3649
Fort Smith, AR 72903
(501) 785-4241

1. Advance Electric Circuits
2. Basic Machine Shop
3. COBOL Programming
4. Digital Circuits
5. Electrical Circuits & Components
6. Fundamentals of Electricity
7. Gen. Welding Appln. & Practice
8. Industrial Electricity
9. Industrial Electricity II
10. Machine Setup & Operations I
11. Machine Setup & Operations II
12. Solid State Components & Circuits
13. Systems Design Implementation
14. Teleprocessing Applications

TOTAL SUBURBAN   167

LOCATION	COLLEGE NAME	COURSE TITLE
URBAN	Anchorage Community College 2533 Providence Ave. Anchorage, AK 99508 (907) 786-1654	1. Business English Review 2. Interpersonal Skills in Office 3. Stress Management 4. Women in Business & Management
	Community College of Allegheny County 800 Allegheny Ave. Pittsburgh, PA 15233 (412) 323-2323	1. A.C. Circuits 2. Advance Comp. Programming 3. Apprenticeship Training 4. Basic Electronics 5. Basic Welding 6. Combustion Technology 7. Communication Strategies 8. Construction Graphics 9. D.C. Circuits 10. Defining Goals & Objectives 11. Electric Instrumentation 12. Electrical Code 13. Electronics 14. Estimating Construction Charges 15. FCC License 16. Heating & Air Conditioning 17. Hospital Cost Accounting 18. Hydraulics 19. Inservice Training for Mechanic 20. Interviewing Skills 21. Intro. to Computers 22. Keyboard Mastery 23. Management Training 24. Microcomputers 25. Microprocessing 26. Millwright 27. Mine Safety 28. Motivation 29. Motor Winding 30. Multimedia First Aid 31. Organizational Conflicts 32. Personal Investment 33. Programmable Controllers 34. Refrigeration & Air Conditioning 35. Scientific Programming I 36. Scientific Programming II 37. Soldering

LOCATION	COLLEGE NAME	COURSE TITLE
		38. Statistics for Quality Control
		39. Strategic Planning
		40. Stress Management
		41. Team Building
		42. Technical Writing
		43. Time Management
		44. Upgrad Heating, A.C. & Elec.
		45. Upgrad Skills of Prod. Workers
		46. Welding
	Community College of Philadelphia 1700 Spring Garden Street Philadelphia, PA 19130 (215) 751-8029	1. Accounting Seminars
		2. American Sign Language
		3. Assertiveness for Managers
		4. Basic Expository Writing
		5. Business Communications
		6. Comm. Skills for Ward Clerks
		7. Communication Skills
		8. Customer Relations
		9. Data Entry Tech.
		10. Driver/Passenger Skills
		11. Management Training
		12. Medical Terminology
		13. Overview of Gerontology
		14. Secretarial Development
		15. Security Training
		16. Word Processing
	Community College of Spokane N. 1810 Greene Street Spokane, WA 99203 (509) 459-3779	1. Basic Electronics
		2. Blueprint Reading
		3. Business Correspondence
		4. Conducting Effective Meetings
		5. Hydraulics
		6. Interpersonal Relations
		7. Keyboarding
		8. Library Tech.
		9. Production Inventory & Control
		10. Statistics for Engineers
		11. Stress Management
		12. Supervisory Training
		13. Teamwork in Organizations
		14. Technical Writing

LOCATION	COLLEGE NAME	COURSE TITLE
		15. Television Prod. Tech.
		16. Visual Media Tech.
		17. Welding
		18. Written Communications
	Central Piedmont Community College P.O. Box 35009 Charlotte, NC 28235 (704) 373-6633	1. Blueprint Reading 2. Bread & Roll Cook 3. Communication Skills 4. Food Preparation Training 5. Housekeeper 6. Individual Referral 7. Machine Operator 8. Material Handling 9. Packaging/Crating 10. Quality Control 11. Secretarial Training 12. Shop Math
	Cuyahoga Community College 700 Carnegie Avenue Cleveland, OH 44115 (216) 348-4776	1. Career Skills Development 2. Clerical Training for Dis. Work 3. Job Search Workshops 4. Placement Counseling 5. Training in Office Procedures
	Eastern Iowa Community College 2804 Eastern Avenue Davenport, IA 52803 (319) 322-5015	1. Accounting 2. Action Skills for Productivity 3. Air Con. & Refrigeration 4. Assembler I 5. BASIC 6. Comm. Skills for Supervisors 7. Effect. Mgmt. Practices 1,2,3 8. Electronics 9. IBM-PC Orientation 10. Intro. to Business 11. Intro. to Small Bus. Computers 12. Lotus 1-2-3 13. Management & Supervision 14. Welding
	El Paso Community College P.O. Box 20500 El Paso, TX 79998 (915) 534-4038	1. Advanced Maintenance 2. Advanced Management 3. Basic Maintenance 4. Basic Pipe Fitting 5. Basic Trade Math 6. Blueprint Reading 7. Business Law

93

LOCATION	COLLEGE NAME	COURSE TITLE
		8. Business Math
		9. Consumer Math
		10. ESL Literacy
		11. ESL Oral Language
		12. ESL Writing
		13. Intro. to Data Processing
		14. Intro. to Psychology
		15. Paint Tech.
		16. Personal Discovery
		17. Personal Finance
		18. Plastic Mold Injection
		19. Precision Instrument Measurement
		20. Principles of Management
		21. Quality Assurance Technician
		22. Sub-Assembling & Deburning
		23. Tool & Die
	Fashion Institute of Technology 227 West 27th Street New York, NY 10001 (212) 760-7672	1. Apparel Manufacturing
		2. Apparel Specification
		3. BASIC
		4. Buyer Training Workshop
		5. Fashion Basic Workshop
		6. Grooming Workshop
		7. Imports Workshop
		8. Knit Sweaters Workshop
		9. Leather Goods Workshop
		10. Management Institute
		11. Merchandise Trends Workshop
		12. Motion & Time Study Seminar
		13. Orientation to Textiles
		14. Pattern Making Concept
		15. Production Manager Workshop
		16. Retail Marketing
		17. Retail Math Workshop
		18. Special Woven Workshop
		19. Textile Apparel Workshop
		20. The ABC's of Advertising
		21. Visual Merchandising Workshop

LOCATION	COLLEGE NAME	COURSE TITLE
	Florida Junior College 101 West State Street Jacksonville, FL 32202 (904) 633-8284	1. Auto Machine Shop 2. Blueprint Reading 3. Carpentry 4. Industrial Electronics 5. Industrial Supervision 6. Industrial Safety 7. Machine Shop 8. Millwright 9. Pipe Fitting 10. Pre-employment Training 11. Supervision 12. Welding
	Metropolitan Community College 3822 Summit Road Kansas City, MO 64111 (816) 756-0220	1. Advanced Blueprint Reading 2. Advanced Sign Language 3. Allied Health Training 4. Assembler 5. Auditor Training 6. Automated Office Skills 7. Bankruptcy 8. Basic Telecommunications 9. Beauty & Skin Care 10. Blueprint Reading 11. Business Law 12. Business Writing 13. Certified Hotel Administration 14. Certified Medication Tech. 15. Clerical Office Training 16. Climate Control 17. Communication 18. Computer Applications in Bus. 19. Computer Familiarization 20. Computer Literacy 21. Computer Operator's Training 22. Computer Systems Training 23. Computerized Bookkeeping 24. Cost Analysis/Bidding 25. Customer Relations 26. Customized Training 27. Data Entry 28. Dealer Management 29. Dental Assistant Training 30. Distribution Techniques 31. Effective Business Writing

LOCATION	COLLEGE NAME	COURSE TITLE
		32. Emergency Medication Tech.
		33. Employee Development
		34. Employee Mgmt. Training
		35. Employee Upgrade Program
		36. Entrepreneurship Seminar
		37. Fast Food Service Training
		38. Fire Prevention
		39. GM Automotive Familiarization
		40. GM Computer Control Systems
		41. IBM PC Training
		42. Insulin Training
		43. Intergraphic Systems
		44. International Trade
		45. Investing in Oil Seminar
		46. Keyboarding
		47. Lead Cook Training
		48. Letter Writing
		49. Litigation, Estate, Probate Law
		50. Lotus 1-2-3
		51. Machinist Training
		52. Management Internship
		53. Management Supervision
		54. Management Training
		55. Manufacturing Process Overview
		56. Marketing and Salesmanship
		57. Medical Transcriptionist
		58. Medical Terminology
		59. Mgmt. LPN Nurses Training
		60. Microcomputer Programming
		61. Northland Leadership
		62. Operating & Profitable Bank
		63. Paramedic Workshop
		64. Problem Solving
		65. Processing Fee for State Fund
		66. Production Skills
		67. Proofreading
		68. Report Writing
		69. Retraining of Personnel
		70. Robotic Training
		71. Sales Relations

LOCATION	COLLEGE NAME	COURSE TITLE
		72. Salesmanship
		73. Secretarial Training
		74. Shorthand
		75. Sign Language
		76. Social Service Designee
		77. Stress Management
		78. Supervision
		79. Supervisory Training
		80. Supervisory Warehouse Mgmt.
		81. Systems Design
		82. Telephone System Training
		83. Telephone Usage Training
		84. Time Management
		85. Train the Trainer
		86. Training Consultation
		87. Training in Thin File
		88. Training in Wafer Prep.
		89. Venture Capital
		90. Waitress Training
		91. Wang Glossary
		92. Wang Word Processing Training
		93. Women Re-Entry
		94. Word Processing
		95. Word Star
		96. Writing and Speech
	Metropolitan Technical Community College P.O. Box 3777 Omaha, NE 68103 (402) 449-8417	1. Arc, Oxy, & Acetylene Welding
		2. Automatic Transmission
		3. Basic Interior Decoration
		4. Basic Supervision
		5. Boiler Operation
		6. Blueprint Reading & Schematics
		7. Computer Literacy
		8. Computers for Data Entry Instrn.
		9. Electrical Maintenance
		10. Elements of Mechanics & Lubri.
		11. Environmental Controls
		12. Equip. Instln. & Sheet Metal Layer
		13. Heavy Equipment Maintenance
		14. House Keeping Tech.

LOCATION	COLLEGE NAME	COURSE TITLE
		15. Industrial Hydraulics
		16. Machine Shop
		17. Nuclear Plant Welding Training
		18. Oral Communication
		19. Piping Systems and Pumps
		20. Plumbing Maintenance
		21. Technical Math & Measurement
		22. Welding
		23. Welding Safety
		24. Written Communication
	Miami-Dade Community College 950 N.W. 20th Street Miami, FL 33127 (304) 347-4133	1. Accounting Principles
		2. Analyzing Financial Statement
		3. Banking & Business Courses
		4. Business Writing
		5. Business/Professional Speaking
		6. Comp. Asst. Design Drafting Workshop
		7. Computer Literacy
		8. Computerized Accounting
		9. Condor Programming
		10. Conversation
		11. Counseling Skills for Managers
		12. Credit Administration
		13. Cultural Anthropology
		14. D-Base II Programming
		15. Emergency Medical Technician
		16. Financial Services
		17. Funeral Services Courses
		18. Humanities
		19. Improving Employee Performances
		20. Improving Managerial Skills
		21. Intro. to Elevator Electronics
		22. Introduction to Data Processing
		23. Introduction to Electronics
		24. Introduction to Engineering
		25. Introduction to Microcomputers

LOCATION	COLLEGE NAME	COURSE TITLE
		26. Lotus 1-2-3
		27. Lotus 1-2-3 Advanced
		28. Lotus 1-2-3 Intermediate
		29. Leadership & Management Skills
		30. Management
		31. Management Development Program
		32. Management Supervision
		33. Managing Your Time
		34. Marketing/Bankers
		35. Medical Terminology
		36. Multiplan Processing
		37. Nat. Inst. of Food Certification
		38. Nursery Principles & Practices
		39. Optimum Performance
		40. Paramedic Training
		41. Pensions & Retirement
		42. Perform. Appraisal & Discpl. Action
		43. Principles & Practices of Market
		44. Principles of Economics
		45. Public Speaking Skills for Executives
		46. Statistics for Behavioral Soc. Sci.
		47. Stress Management
		48. Survey of Management
		49. Symphony Processing
		50. Team Building
		51. Technical Math
		52. The Living Computer
		53. Understanding Motivation & Work
		54. Water Treatment Plant Operator
		55. Writing Development

LOCATION	COLLEGE NAME	COURSE TITLE
	Minneapolis Community College 1501 Hennepin Ave. Minneapolis, MN 55409 (612) 341-7022	1. Business Courses
	Portland Comm. Coll. 12000 S.W. 49th Ave. Portland, OR 97219 (503) 244-6111	1. Business Letter Writing 2. CPR 3. Computer Drafting 4. Coding Medical Records 5. Correction Case Worker 6. Customer Relations 7. Electronics 8. Emergency Medical Tech. 9. Fire Arson Investigation 10. Management 11. Phlebotomy 12. Refrigeration 13. Technical Report Writing 14. Welding
	Rancho Santiago Community College 17th and Bristol Streets Santa Ana, CA 92706 (714) 667-3497	1. Automated Stock Control Clerk 2. Comm. Skills for Engineers 3. Computer-Aided Drafting 4. Computerized Machine Operator 5. Coordinated Design Decision 6. Diesel Mechanic/Technician 7. Materials Requirements Planning Optr. 8. Senior Test Technician
	Sinclair Community College 444 West Third Street Dayton, OH 45402 (513) 226-2854	1. Accounting 2. Business Law 3. Computer-Assisted Design I, II 4. Computer Concepts 5. Computer Literacy 6. Electronic Workshop 7. Geometric Tolerancing 8. Industrial Management 9. Marketing 10. Management Principles 11. Portfolio Development 12. Rapid Editing 13. Stress Management

LOCATION	COLLEGE NAME	COURSE TITLE
	State Technical Institute at Knoxville P.O. Box 19802 5908 Lyons View Drive Knoxville, TN 37939-2802 (615) 584-6103	1. Accounting 2. Basic Electricity 3. Blueprint Reading 4. D-Base Programming 5. Digital Electronics 6. Electrical Maintenance 7. Electronics 8. Financial Management 9. Gearing Maintenance 10. Hydraulics I, II, III 11. Introduction to Microcomputers 12. Mechanical Maintenance 13. Shaft Alignment
	Valencia Community College P.O. Box 3028 Orlando, FL 32802 (305) 299-5000	1. Accounting 2. Accounting 1 & 2 3. Business Math 4. Communications 5. Comp. Prog. for Severely Disabled 6. Computer Literacy 7. Congestive Heart 8. Credit Union Operations 9. Critical Care Nursing 10. Data Processing 11. Dealing with Angry Customers 12. Death/Dying 13. EKG Monitoring/ Interpretation 14. Elected Officials Instruction 15. I.V. Therapy 16. Infection Control 17. Interviewing & Documenting 18. Keyboard Mastery 19. Keyboarding 20. Mastery Teaching 21. Management Communications 22. Performance Appraisals 23. Principles of Economics 24. Report Writing 25. Salesmanship 26. Stress Management 27. Supervision

LOCATION	COLLEGE NAME	COURSE TITLE
		28. Supervisory Skills for Gov't Employees
		29. Time Management
		30. Typing Skills
		31. Word Processing

TOTAL URBAN		426
TOTAL ALL COLLEGES		651

02000043

70142

DATE DUE
